Finding Anthony

Defeating Autism with Verbal Behavior, Biomedical Treatments, and Other Alternatives

By Christie Burnett

Forward by
Dr. James A. Neubrander, M.D.

Aspiring Angels Therapy, LLC 2008

Finding Anthony: Defeating Autism with Verbal Behavior,
Biomedical Treatments, and Other Alternatives
copyright © 2008, Christie Burnett
foreword copyright © 2008, Dr. James A. Neubrander

All rights reserved. No part of this book may be reproduced or transmitted in any form or by any means, electronic or mechanical, including photocopying, recording, or any information storage, retrieval or transmission system without permission in writing from the Author.

ISBN #: 978-0-578-00137-1

Published by:
Lulu Publishing Company
www.lulu.com

Aspiring Angels Therapy, LLC
1 Harrison Road
Kinnelon, NJ 07405
973-296-1894
info@aspiringangels.net

Nothing in this book should be construed as medical advice. Exercises, therapies, diets, supplements, drugs, or any other actions, materials or devices described herein should only be used when the reader has consulted professionals in those fields. The advice of health care professionals, educators, nutritionists and practitioners in other relevant areas should be heeded.

DEDICATION

I dedicate this book to all the families and children still battling the world of Autism. I believe that all your hard work, devotion, sacrifice, and dedication will pay off for your children. Keep holding on! **BELIEVE** in recovery! God bless all of you. Christie

ANTHONY BEFORE RECOVERY

(He would hold a spoon in each hand 24/7)

Finding Anthony - Table of Contents

Introduction	7
Chapter 1 – The Disappearing Child	11
Observations: Antibiotics and Vaccines	19
Chapter 2 – Naming the Monster	22
Observations – Early Intervention	29
Chapter 3 – Do Or Diet	30
Observations: Leaky Gut Syndrome & GFCF	39
Chapter 4 – Anthony on Trial	43
Observations: History of Autism & ABA	51
Chapter 5 – Officially Diagnosed:	
A Look Inside A Little Boy	54
Chapter 6 – Saboteurs, Support and Saviors	67
Chapter 7 – Verbal Behavior: A Manding Miracle	74
Observations: ABLLS, Pairing and Manding	87
Chapter 8 – A Glass of Milk, A Cup of Poison	94
Observations: Sign Language in VB	104

Chapter 9 – Discovering Dapper DAN   111
    Observations: Dr. N & M-B12   127
Chapter 10 – Methyl-B12: A Microscopic Miracle   130
    Observations – M-B12 and VB Combo   138

Chapter 11 – Getting The VB Ball Rolling   139
    Observations: VB Workshops and Resources   149
Chapter 12 – Old Team, New Therapies   150
    Observations: VB Tools and Techniques   158
Chapter 13 – Mommy Breaks Down, Mommy Rises Up   161
    Observations: DAN Conference and SCD Diet   176
Chapter 14 – Healing Guts and Helping Strangers   181
    Observations – Diet & Supplements   188
Chapter 15 – Dr. Know-It-All Knows Nothing   190
Chapter 16 – The Next Step: Getting VB in Schools   201
Chapter 17 - VB for All: A Bureaucratic Battle   210
Chapter 18 –Diagnosis Lost:
    A Snow Angel Spreads His Wings   218

Appendix
Daily Routines and Calendar Events   225
Jimmy's Story   234

FOREWORD
By Dr. James A. Neubrander, M.D.

The best way to teach is to show, and the best way to show is with a story. This is a mystery story. Its villain is a disease, and its victim is a little boy, Anthony. Like most villains, this one lurks in the darkness. More than that, it *is* the darkness, which makes finding the clues all the more difficult. For that you need a detective who is intrepid and passionate. Our detective, Christie Burnett, is both of those things.

The mystery she had to solve had taken her son, Anthony. It was as if her child of less than a year had gone missing, even though his body was still right there. Autism severed the connection between Anthony and the world around him, Christie understood the goal of her detective work from the start: to restore that connection. Anthony's story became the central focus of his family, and touched many others as well, including me. I am a physician and I treat children with autism every day. That has been my part in Anthony's story.

Early on in my relationship with the Burnetts, Christie and her husband, Don, took a page from the TV show "Seinfeld," and began referring to me as the "Soup Nazi." One could take offense, but I didn't. The nickname came from my lengthy requests for detailed information about their son's health. I ask for a great deal from parents with autistic children, and a little kidding about it doesn't bother me. These parents know from experience that I'm nowhere near as demanding as the disease itself. I ask for parents to be acute observers ("strategic scientists" as

Christie might say) so that all of us might help these children recover.

"Autism" is a word that's been on everyone's lips lately. There's good reason. In recent decades autism's increase has been huge, with at least six times as many cases being reported. Each case is a child falling into the darkness. Many possible causes have been cited for this general trend, but only a story of real people can show the human toll, and inspire each of us to play our parts in solving the mystery.

In "Finding Anthony" Christie maps the journey that she and her family have taken in their efforts to put the puzzle together, and defeat autism in Anthony. She includes the struggles and heartbreak, as well as the victories and cheers. It is the story of a mother and a family that have done everything humanly possible to recover a child from autism's numbing grip. Christie is a fighter who has proved unwilling to allow official skepticism, arrogance or disbelief to stand in her way.

More than that, as Christie helped her son battle this disease, she never lost her sensitivity to others in similar plights. She knew that this struggle must also be waged on a larger front, where all parents work together. She recognized how vital it was to link the autistic community—parents, doctors, therapists and teachers—all in service to the goal of helping every child affected with autism. She learned that dealing with autism meant attacking it on every front with every effective tool available, using medical, educational and therapeutic methods. She was not afraid to try things, and once she saw something that worked she stuck with it, no matter what the skeptics said.

In doing this, Christie was forming a whole approach. It included diet, supplements and biomedical treatments (which is what brought her to me). It also employed Verbal Behavior methods developed by B.F. Skinner and his successors. She encouraged Anthony's therapists to learn these methods with her. This helped with the everyday identification of wants and needs that most of us take for granted. She knew that the same processes would be necessary as Anthony entered school, so that he could progress, and eventually join all the other children in a normal life. The nuts-and-bolts of those processes are here with the story, contained in the *Observations* section at the end of each chapter. These sections give readers a fuller understanding of the methods covered in the story. They are clues to the mystery's solution.

As I've noted, recovering a child from autism requires the help of many. Christie got that help, and now she knows that she has a duty to assist others. She does it well. With her helpers at Aspiring Angels, Christie gives hope and real quality of life to autistic children and their families. In the course of these efforts she has put her approach in action. It requires dedication and hard work. If you take this journey, and wind up with a doctor like me, you might find yourself recording details late into the night, while muttering about Soup Nazis. I hope you say it with at least a chuckle, and I hope you read this book from cover-to-cover. This story is a suspenseful puzzle any reader will want to solve, and it is also a gold mine of useful information. If you, or anyone you know, are facing the challenges of autism, this book will help you persevere and triumph.

Finding Anthony ~ Christie Burnett

CHAPTER ONE

My youngest son, Anthony, was about eight months old when I first suspected how deep our problem was. Not that I put a name to it. If we can possibly avoid naming a disease or condition we usually do. The lump in the skin doesn't immediately translate to "cancer," nor does the twinge in the arm make us clutch for our hearts. We detour around disturbances, and don't talk about them, even to ourselves. Anthony had been through a particularly rough month of illness and doctor visits. Now that he was better, we wanted to believe this was just a bump in the road.

So I thought up a surprise for my husband Don. Now that Anthony was older, I would take a picture of our three sunny kids smiling at him, for his office. I had the perfect place, a daisy patch, in mind. A few weeks earlier I'd driven by a spot full of wildflowers edged by daisies. I waited for the perfect day, then dressed Austin, who was seven, Daniella, just past two, and Anthony. I posed them in the flowers, taking time out between shots to say: "Over here, Austin... wait, let's try Daniella down here..." and to also reposition Anthony.

"Anthony, look at me," I said. Peering into the viewfinder, I suddenly realized how many times I'd said that. I felt a split second of fear, a shiver, then I shook it off.

And it didn't occur to me then. Not really. Not yet.

"Anthony, come on. Look at Mommy."

I went through two rolls of film. Sometimes one kid would make a face, or another would duck into the flowers. But not one shot had Anthony looking at the camera, although I'd made silly noises and clapped my hands.

A few days later as I sorted through the prints with my mother, I asked: "Which one do you think is best?" She'd already examined each one. Now she went through the stack as if they were playing cards.

"It's really hard to pick," she said. "Anthony just didn't want to look at the camera, did he?"

"No," I admitted. "He really wasn't into it." It was then I felt the shiver, as if I'd let something slip out I didn't want to talk about.

"Had he had a bad night?" she asked.

"I'm not sure," I said.

The moment passed. The shiver was nothing but memory. I had a son, and his family loved him.

Those last parts were true.

But the shiver wasn't just a memory.

It would return again and again in the coming months. It followed Anthony's empty stares. People noticed that Anthony was the quiet boy, the good boy—too good. Often he simply didn't react to things like other children. At the playground he often sat alone. At times I wondered if this child was learning anything at all.

Through ear infections, constipation, and one prescription after another, I found myself wondering: what is happening to my son? He'd been normal the day he was born, and for months afterward. What was happening? I couldn't piece together all the parts in the puzzle, but I felt as if they added up to that: the loss of something vital, something that had been there, but was now ebbing. I had never experienced a fear that had grown so slowly and stayed for so long.

Then came a day when I could give the fear a name: Autism. A basic article of faith of our age is that identifying a problem is the first step to solving it. This didn't feel that way at all. The word "autism" seemed like nothing more than a synonym for "fear."

With the word out in the open, I looked at my son, and knew I had to go on. I was just as afraid as I had been before, but I knew that if I didn't try to get us over this obstacle something would die in Anthony, a life force that I was sure was still there. And if that happened something would die in me, and in my family.

I was looking at a mystery far more horrific than those we find in novels. Anthony's mind was suffocating. If he was ever going to have anything close to a normal life, I had to find a way for his mind to breathe.

***

The daisy patch was the first moment that I began the process of identifying what was wrong. What made it hard was letting go of my image of my little boy. I could remember barely three months earlier, when my mother-in-law, Lucy, flew in for the weekend. We were all excited about Lucy's visit. It would be the first meeting between her and her new grandson.

On that quiet moment on Saturday morning, Lucy first experienced her grandson. We sat on the floor in our den, surrounded by toys. She held Anthony, then set him down. I could see she was entranced. So was he.

Anthony watched her. Looking at his eyes, I saw an infant taking in a whole world for the first time. It was what he was doing every day, and now here was this wonderful new person, loving him. "He's a flirt," Lucy said.

"What?"

"He's already a flirt. Aren't you, Anthony?" She gave him a sudden stare, and popped her eyes wide. Anthony crinkled his button-nose and smiled bashfully at her.

It was real bashfulness, not just the involuntary reflexes of muscles. Anthony gave a sigh. I heard pleasure in it.

"You see, our Anthony is already flirting with the girls. Who taught him that?" She looked at me, raising an eyebrow. I shrugged. We both laughed.

At five months my son was already growing up.

***

When our children are born, we look for all the signs of normality. In that first moment we want to see all the right things. Even with the squeezed shut eyes, and the shiny body unfolding in the world for the first time, we look for the obvious: two arms, two legs, fingers, toes, ears and all the rest. We want to know our baby is perfect, the way a baby ought to be.

Anthony was our third. He arrived in November of 2001.

Before I left for the hospital, my oldest son, Austin, stood in the doorway watching. He wore a troubled look. "When will you be back home?" he asked.

"Soon," I said. "Don't worry, Aust."

Austin fidgeted. He had the blond hair and blue eyes of a fair young child, but always found a way to worry. Some kids are carefree. Austin was six-going-on-sixty and had already earned the nickname "Gramps." He could be so empathetic and responsible, but I still wished he could relax and enjoy being a child.

"Take it easy, Aust," I said, latching my suitcase. "Come over here." I hugged him, then rubbed his back. "I brought your sister home all right. Now I'll bring this one, and once he's here you'll be a big help, just like you always are."

"Yeah," he said. "I will."

Austin's younger sister, Daniella, was just the opposite. Resembling me at every turn, at only twenty months she already showed more than her share of spunk and spark. My second child didn't accept "no" easily. Being outgoing was a help, but I sometimes wondered if Daniella and I were too stubborn for our own good.

Those thoughts crossed my mind as I walked out to the car. I was having the birth induced, and though I was looking forward to seeing my newborn boy, I wasn't looking forward to the process. The pain of my first labor was a memory that could put a knot in my stomach.

"Your mom will be there soon," Don said as we neared the hospital, reassuring me. Between friends and family I didn't have much to worry about.

At 1:52 PM that afternoon a seven-pound baby boy was born. Finally I met this little guy who had been kicking, punching and rolling around inside of me. He was perfect.

Don fell for him too, staring at every inch of his new son, finding him to be right in every way. As promised, my mom was there, and once I'd finished inspecting my son, I handed him to her. She wrapped him in a blanket and cried as only a mother can. Austin and Daniella came in later, thrilled to meet their new brother. All five of us squeezed onto the hospital bed for a family picture.

We named him Anthony Donald. With thick dark hair, olive skin and brown eyes, Anthony resembled my Panamanian mother-in-law. One afternoon about seven weeks later I picked Anthony up, and he felt as if he were burning. His temperature was well above normal. It scared me. I thought of a dear friend who had lost her two-year-old granddaughter to meningitis. Terrified, I called the hospital. They said to bring him in if the fever went above 101°. I stayed up all night.

The next morning our pediatrician said Anthony had an ear infection. It was January and this was the season for such illness. I had just enrolled Daniella in preschool. For three mornings a week she would be exposed to dozens of other kids, and every germ in New Jersey. Would she get sick and pass colds and viruses on to Anthony?

That morning my seven-week-old received his first antibiotics.

Two mornings later I noticed a pull in Anthony's ribcage. I was giving him a bath when I saw the signs. His was breathing fast, and with every inhalation I could see his ribs. It looked as if he had a vacuum in his ribcage drawing the skin tight.

I made a panicky call to my cousin Sharon. She ran over to our house in her pajamas and slippers and watched him for a couple of minutes.

"Yes, he's really having to pull to breathe," she said. The pediatrician's office was closed. Again, I watched him closely through the night, dismayed by his breathing and the fact that he couldn't relax.

The next day our pediatrician gave me a nebulizer and showed me how to give him a breathing treatment.

Finally his fever broke. The doctor said Anthony had RSV, a respiratory virus, and should get better. Sure enough, he seemed all right within a couple days. I wanted to think the worst was over.

In the months that followed we became regulars at the pediatrician's office. Anthony came down with an ear infection about once a month. The solution always seemed to be another course of antibiotics. Again and again I carried the slips to the pharmacy, getting a bottle of pills in return.

I wonder if any mother gives her child doses from our modern cornucopia of drugs without feeling some qualms. I didn't want my baby to be sick, but I was also aware that antibiotics can upset the balance in an adult body. Couldn't they create greater problems for a baby? I was concerned, but more concerned about relieving my child's pain. And this was the recommended course.

Because modern medicine dictates that children get their vaccinations at certain months, Anthony sometimes got vaccinated when he was already fighting a cold or virus. When I asked if that was safe the doctors and nurses reassured me. "He's had so much to deal with," I would say.

"He looks okay," they would reply. "As long as he doesn't have a fever, he'll be fine."

It didn't rest well with me. How much could his body fight off at one time?

Though my preference was to hold off on the vaccines until Anthony was older, I took the strong suggestions of the doctors. Theirs was the conventional wisdom, and wasn't that supposed to be the safe bet? Did I want to risk some greater disease?

Yet I knew that insisting on so many vaccines had not always been so accepted. Although Austin was only six years older than Anthony, we hadn't subjected his immune system to the hepatitis shot, or Prevnar, chicken pox and flu shots. Over the course of my children's infancies, I'd seen a number of new vaccines added to a baby's standard schedule.

Austin had gotten a few ear infections but they hadn't started until he was about eighteen months. Yet I wasn't as focused on Anthony's ear infections as I was on his breathing problems. When a child can't breathe, it scares you. Don and I spent too many nights watching Anthony suffer this way. It would begin with a strange cough—a sound I will never forget.

It usually started after dinner. Anthony would start grunting, then coughing, then growling, finally erupting into a scream. It sounded like violent attempts to clear his throat. We would treat him with the nebulizer, then let him sleep sitting up in his stroller. By morning his voice would be gone. When he opened his mouth, his throat straining, there was only a terrible, pathetic silence.

The pediatrician said he had Reactive Airway disease, an infantile form of asthma, and gave him steroids. Again and again I would describe the evening cough, but it seemed beyond his doctors' comprehension. Although I was sure something was different about this cough, I could not convey it. I never heard a wheeze. The dearth of answers, and the cough's persistence frustrated me more and more. Did the doctors take anything I said seriously? Was even my family beginning to think I was being an alarmist?

When Anthony was seven months old, we went on vacation to the beach with my parents, brothers, sister-in-laws and niece. We stayed together in one big house. It was a trip I'd looked forward to. I felt like it had been far too long since I'd hung out with my family on the beach and boardwalk.

On the second day Anthony started getting sick. That afternoon he felt warm to me and I feared his coughing was about to begin again. That evening, after we put Anthony to bed, my family members were sitting within earshot of the baby monitor. It wasn't long before the peculiar sounds started. First it was a cough, then growling, then screaming: "UHH-RRR! UHH-RRR!" This didn't sound like a child at all. It had depth, as if we were hearing a cough from the lungs of a grown man. Though he was desperate for sleep, the cough kept jarring him awake.

The noise of it cut to the core of me.

I ran upstairs and did a breathing treatment with the nebulizer, but it didn't help. I knew he needed steroids.

My mother was upset. "Isn't there something you can do for him?" she asked.

"I don't know," I said. "I just don't know."

My sister-in-law sat next to the monitor. "How awful," she breathed. "How very awful."

In that moment my family saw the torture that we had been dealing with. My mother insisted we take him to the ER. We drove there with Anthony coughing. In the waiting room he drew everyone's attention. He was the loudest one there.

"What's wrong with that baby?" a little girl asked her mom. "Why is he making those noises?"

After a wait they took us into the back where a doctor examined him. "Is it possible that something could have lodged in his throat?" the doctor asked. "Maybe a pen cap or a coin, or something off the floor?"

"I don't think so," I said. "This is chronic.

Up to now steroids have helped."

The doctor insisted on an X-ray. It didn't turn anything up. "It could still be a blockage down there," he said. "I want you to take the X-rays to your son's pulmonologist, and tell them I've suggested a scope of his airway and lungs."

He had also found that Anthony had another ear infection which meant my baby would get yet another round of antibiotics.

CHAPTER OBSERVATIONS

I have mentioned vaccines in this chapter, and recent history indicates that the loaded schedule of vaccinations, and the presence of mercury in some of them, have played a part in the spread of autism. We will explore this relationship further in future chapters. The ideas concerning this relationship are based on the effects vaccines can have on a baby's immune system. Antibiotics also affect the immune system. This is true for all of us, but a baby's fragile immune system is especially at risk

I remember when I first read about antibiotics playing a role in the possible causes of autism. At several points I felt as if I was literally reading my son's story. In the gut we find various bacteria, both "good" and "bad." Antibiotics kill all bacteria. Without "good" bacteria, excess yeast grows in the gastrointestinal tract. The good bacteria try to build up again, but if yeast overwhelms them, another bad bug invades and causes an infection. Doctors prescribe more antibiotics. More antibiotics mean more yeast, further weakening a baby's overworked immune system. This is a recipe for more ear infections.

Many autistic children suffer chronic respiratory and ear infections. Anthony had both. These children have a biochemical disorder which is linked to an inability to detoxify their bodies of toxins and heavy metals. Jacquelyn McCandless (author and Defeat Autism Now [DAN] doctor) writes in her book "Children with Starving Brains" about autistic children who have poor immune systems, poor digestion, and poor absorption of nutrients. Months later, when I read her book, I took note of the bowel issues these children had. Diarrhea and constipation were common among them. At that point, when Anthony was still having severe problems with his bowels, I guessed he had a faulty immune system. Every cold he had turned into a nasty ear infection followed by an asthma attack.

Too many antibiotics can damage the gut, which is why Anthony had so many bowel problems. Anthony had been on antibiotics since he'd been seven weeks old.

Once again, antibiotics kill all bacteria, but do not harm yeast, which is kept at bay by "good" bacteria. When the yeast outnumbers the good bacteria the immune system suffers. (This is similar to why women get vaginal yeast infections while on antibiotics and need to eat yogurt. The yogurt has the good bacteria in it and keeps the yeast from growing.)

Yeast is a fungus called Candida Albicans. Behavior problems such as aggression, hyperactivity, short attention span, and lethargy have been linked to yeast overgrowth.

Yeast can be harmful to your health, causing headaches, fatigue, depression, stomach aches, and constipation. Yeast releases toxins into the body which affect the immune system as well as the neurological system. For more information on yeast read "The Candida Yeast-Autism Connection" by Dr. Stephen M. Edelson.

CHAPTER TWO

A few weeks later, at seven months old, Anthony was scoped.

Don was leaving on a business trip that day, and I had to go through most of it alone. It was new to me. Neither Austin nor Daniella had ever had to go through anything quite like this. I held Anthony as they pushed in the IV to sedate him. I watched as his eyes rolled back.

Once Anthony was out the medical people went to work. I waited in another room. About a half hour later the doctor came out. He said Anthony was doing well.

"I think we may have some answers," he said. "Your son has laryngeal malasia, which is a floppy epiglottis."

"What's that mean?" I asked.

He pointed to his throat. "The epiglottis is about here, at the mouth of the windpipe. It's a cartilage plate that covers the windpipe when you swallow. Anthony's is enlarged and floppy so when he gets one of these asthma attacks it gives him a choking sensation. That's why he gets that cough. We could do laser surgery but then there's a chance of scar tissue in the throat."

When I heard that I thought of our cocker spaniel. Years ago she got into something that left her with irreversible scar tissue in her throat. Ever since then she couldn't eat anything solid. If a piece of meat fell to the floor she'd eat it and vomit it up within ten seconds.

"No thanks," I said to the idea of surgery.

"Okay. Well, we can put him on an asthma medication to limit the attacks."

"I'd rather do that," I said.

More drugs. I didn't like it, but I felt it was a choice between that and risky surgery. Anthony started taking high dosage asthma meds twice a day. They helped the cough but not his ear infections.

A month later we were back at the hospital. This time he went under general anesthesia. They were putting tubes in his ears in the hope of ending his ear infections.

"He gets these because fluid gets trapped in his ears," the doctor had told me.

"Would it help if I changed his formula from cow's milk to soy?" I asked.

The doctor looked at me as if I were speaking gibberish.

"I just thought, well, cow's milk makes my saliva feel thicker," I said. "Wouldn't it thicken the fluid? Wouldn't that make it more prone to getting trapped there?"

"Oh," the doctor said, nodding, "right. In this case I don't think it'll make much difference. We just need to clean it out. That's all."

"But if his fluids had a thinner consistency..."

"Just let us try this," he said.

So they put tubes in his ears, and, despite their lack of enthusiasm, I switched to soy milk.

Once Anthony had tubes in his ears I could always tell when he had an infection because liquid would ooze out. As far as I could see that was the only benefit. His infections were only a little less frequent. His switch to soy milk did have some clear effects. Within days after he stopped eating dairy foods his eye contact improved. Still, I had a youngest son who was sick most of the time.

By this time it was fall. Anthony would soon have his first birthday. I thought of how hard life had been on him so far, and I began to dread the winter. His life seemed to be an endless succession of visits to doctors, but none of their remedies were working. The tubes in his ears hardly helped at all, and sometimes he seemed to be living on antibiotics.

At nine months I had begun to notice Anthony's pace with learning; he was behind. My family is a big one, and my husband and I are constantly in a world of many babies. We'd already had two before Anthony. At family gatherings Anthony often sat quietly. His eyes would be open, but nothing was going on. Sometimes people commented on how good he was. It was true. He was too good!

"I'm worried," I said to my cousin Kimmy. "Anthony doesn't seem to connect the way Austin and Daniella did."

"Connect how?"

"Connect with me, with Austin and Daniella… with anyone. He just doesn't seem to notice much."

"He's been sick," she said, "and he's getting better. All these illnesses slowed him up. As he gets better he'll catch up. You'll see."

I told myself she was right. I went over to my son, picked him up, and kissed him. He squirmed. He always squirmed when I held him. He hadn't even reacted to the kiss. I set him down, and looked at him. I felt my stomach knot. I wanted to hold my son.

That night, after he was asleep, I went into his room. I picked him up and held his sleeping body. He was quiet. As long as he was asleep he would stay quiet there in my arms. I cried. It wasn't the first time.

Winter approached. The ear infections wouldn't give up. I began to notice him sweating, pushing and straining. After a few times I realized I wasn't finding anything in his diaper. Anthony was constipated. We started to give him enemas. Soon they were a regular routine. We tried prune juice and fruit but nothing helped. The pediatrician put him on Lactulose. It didn't work, but we kept him on it, hoping that it would.

Anthony stopped responding to his name. Was his hearing failing? One evening when Anthony was fooling with a puzzle, Don stood next to him and said his name. When he got no response he leaned in close. "Anthony," he said, louder. Anthony kept looking at the puzzle. Don practically screamed his name. Ant didn't seem to know he was there. He moved one puzzle piece. Don grabbed Anthony's face and turned it towards him. "Anthony. Anthony. Look at me!"

Anthony wanted to turn back to the puzzle. He looked down as if he was intentionally avoiding eye contact. Don straightened up. He said nothing. What was there to say?

When I would look straight at Anthony he would avoid my glance. He would turn his head to the right or left, always away from me. Our feelings of rejection were constant. It was as if our son was receding into another world on purpose. He was ignoring us. He wanted to be held but not hugged. When I held him he couldn't get comfortable. I would set him down. He would cry again. I'd pick him back up and he would squirm. "What does he want?" I thought.

At his first birthday party Anthony wouldn't come out of our bedroom. Whenever we brought him out to see the guests he would cry and scream. We gave in. People went into our bedroom to see him. "The birthday boy is hiding," someone said.

I thought: "He's always hiding."

The other toddlers would run, laugh and chase the older children. Anthony would sit alone in our room. Anthony seemed to be tuning out of our world. He was only happy when left alone to watch TV. He would sit in front of it, mesmerized. Though that is a picture of many normal kids, Anthony's television habits were in a context that didn't include play, or verbal communication. When you saw this child sitting in the soft blue light of the tube, it was as if that was all that was there. It was the only clear, consistent portrait of him. A normal kid sitting, hypnotized by the tube might annoy you, make you angry, or you might even laugh. When I saw Anthony watching TV I felt scared.

Up to that winter Anthony had done some normal things such as "Patty Cake," "Give Me a Kiss," and "How Big is the Baby?" Now even those faded.

I began to question my memory. "He did do those things, didn't he?" I asked Don.

"Yeah, he did them but he just doesn't want to be bothered right now." Don replied.

"But now he never wants to be bothered," I said. "Really, never!"

When Don saw my worry, he worried. People were beginning to realize that something eerie was going on. Anthony had no words and barely any babble. He couldn't wave bye-bye, or point to something he wanted or needed. When he wanted something he simply cried. It was the cry of an infant, but Anthony was fourteen months old.

I spoke to a neighbor who had an autistic child.

"If it's happening, you're going to get a lot of advice," she said. "Every doctor, and every professional, and every friend is going to have their ideas. I'll tell you this: follow your heart, Christie. And act. Whatever you do, do something."

"Some people think I'm paranoid," I said. "They just think Anthony is laid back."

"There are a million comforting clichés," she said. "They'll say he's a third child, or a late bloomer, or whatever. Well, none of us want to think the worst. But you have to. All these problems he's had may be having permanent effects. If they aren't, you won't hurt him. I say: act!"

I needed a voice like hers.

When Anthony was almost fifteen months old I started to research childhood development. Was he hitting his developmental milestones? What I read made me nervous. My son was delayed at best.

My neighbor gave me the phone number for New Jersey's Early Intervention program. This is a state-run program for children ages birth-to-three years old. If a parent thinks a child is having serious difficulties, this agency will send a team of therapists to make an evaluation. If your child is 25% delayed in three developmental areas, or 33% delayed in one area, then you qualify. Trained therapists come into your home and work with your child.

The program wasn't snag-free. It would be some weeks before the therapists would have time to come see us, but I did get Anthony onto their schedule.

In February, at Anthony's fifteen-month check-up I spoke to the doctor about my concerns. She asked if Anthony pointed to his wants and needs. She asked if he could say any words such as Ma ma, Da da, or anything else.

"No," I said. "He doesn't understand language. If I say: 'Where's your cup,' or 'Do nice to the doggie,' or 'Let's go night-night,' he doesn't respond. Most of the time he ignores us, and he never responds to his name."

As she looked at Anthony staring ahead she said: "Yes, that worries me too. I'm not saying anything definitely, but I think it could be PDD. That's Pervasive Developmental Disorder. I want you to take Anthony to a developmental pediatrician to get him evaluated. He should have his hearing checked too. Also, there's a state program for early intervention."

"I've already called them" I said. "We have an appointment set up."

"Good. I'm glad you're already acting on this," she said.

"I had to," I told her. "I couldn't wait."

I wasn't exactly clear on what Pervasive Developmental Disorder was. The name haunted me. The whole process seemed spooky. You talk to a neighbor, and she prods you to call an agency. You read some articles, and identify symptoms. A doctor speaks in the technical tongue of medicine. You hear a phrase, and the initials that go with it. What you don't want to hear is the name of the disease. "PDD" was not quite a name. It wasn't a single, sharp word that could dig deeply into my fears. But I knew the word that I wanted to avoid: Autism. That was the empty stare.

"Maybe it is a hearing problem," I whispered to myself as we left the pediatrician's office.

Then, in my head, I heard my neighbor. "Act!" she had said.

So I made the appointment with the developmental pediatrician. That wouldn't be for another two months: far too much time. I was determined not to wait.

That night Don and I were having a long-planned dinner with a coworker and his wife. As we ate these two told us about their nephew who had been diagnosed with autism. As they described his symptoms, my heart sank. They were painting a picture of my son.

Don and I got home and went on the Internet, starting with a search on autism. There was a checklist test. We answered all the questions and hit "enter." The answer came: "Autism Spectrum Disorder." Suddenly we were both weeping. I sobbed. I ran over to Anthony's crib and looked at him sleeping peacefully. I gently brushed the hair away from his face. "Oh my baby, where are you? You're there; I can feel it, please God, no, no." It felt like the baby I'd thought was there had died.

The word was there now, out in the open, with all its images and fears. The diagnosis wasn't official, but we knew it would be. That night we looked at our baby, and resolved to fight. We would not allow autism to take Anthony unopposed. We would do whatever it took to free him.

CHAPTER OBSERVATIONS

Many parents feel they need to be referred to Early Intervention from their pediatricians. This is not the case and can cause a delay in obtaining services for a child who badly needs them. Thankfully my neighbor explained that I could call and have Anthony evaluated without a doctor's referral. So I made the call. The person I spoke to explained that it would take a month or more for someone to come to evaluate Anthony.

Evaluation and early intervention are key. Though any child can benefit from the methods described in the following chapters, it's always best to start right away. That way you can coordinate the efforts of the EI providers with your own.

The first step is to get a diagnosis you trust, and then act as quickly as possible. It's usually best to start with diet for two reasons: first, you can start it today, and second, within one or two weeks you will probably begin to see results. Diet will affect behavior. As in any long, difficult process, perceptions are key. If you can see an improvement early it can help you endure rough spots later.

Whenever you begin to see problems, take my neighbor's advice to heart. Always be careful, but act! When a child is regressing, every day counts.
The checklist for autistic symptoms is at www.childbrain.com.

CHAPTER THREE

The next day I had a patient scheduled for 7 AM. When I got to work, my coworkers Mary and Michelle took one look at me and said: "What happened?"

"Last night was the worst," I said, and I told them all I could about the previous day and evening. By the time I finished we were all in tears. It wasn't the first time that I found myself thankful for having supportive people to work with.

I worked through my schedule of morning patients, then that afternoon I made the appointment with the developmental pediatricians. They had a crowded calendar, and would not be able to see us until April, over two months away, but I wasn't about to sit and wait. My son was in trouble, and needed help now.

In the next couple of weeks Don and I had Anthony's hearing tested. When the results came back the audiologist was happy.

"Your son's hearing is fine," she said. "He can hear all the normal ranges."

It sounded fine, but deep down I felt almost disappointed. It might have been easier if the problem had been a physical one in his ears. What if it was simply some fluid, or some undiscovered swelling? What if all of these difficulties had stemmed from some simple, barely perceptible growth near his eardrum, something that could be cut out in a moment? There had been those chronic ear infections, and weren't there some incredibly important health issues that hinged on the ear? The sense of balance is there, and the ear is right there by the brain. I yearned for a simple solution: something they could fix with some standard, modern medical procedure. I wanted the magic wand.

Yet I knew deep down that Anthony's healing wouldn't come from any one clear, concise medical action, or from magic. The only question was: where will it come from?

My neighbor had told me to act, and I had called New Jersey's Department of Health and Senior Services. They contracted with early intervention providers to evaluate cases such as Anthony's, and set up the proper programs of therapy. A few weeks after the preliminary diagnosis Early Intervention providers (EI) came to our home for the first time. This initial visit was all about evaluating Anthony. They put him through several kinds of testing, and found that he was more than 33% delayed in three out of five areas, and 25% delayed in a fourth area. The only area where he had advanced as much as a normal boy of sixteen months was in gross motor skills.

Their report put the facts in stark perspective. Numbers are colder than language. They have no euphemisms. Anthony was behind, and now it was there on paper. At sixteen months old he was as advanced as an average six-month-old in expressive and receptive language. Developmentally he was at nine months. In the emotional and cognitive areas he was nine months as well. I read the statistics and felt them draining my hopes. Then I steeled myself. The numbers would simply have to change. My son and I would change them. The providers told us they would begin to work with him soon. I said to myself: "It can't be soon enough."

***

I was beginning to realize that my son and I were running a race. What I didn't yet see was that the race was not simply against the autism that was taking over his brain, it was also a race that involved the history, and present-day perception of the whole of autism. The race is to find out, and put together what is already known, but it is also to be among those who discover more. Every autistic child, and every parent, and every DAN doctor, and every member of the autism community is running both of these races. We aren't running against each other; we're running for each other, and we're striving to learn everything we can. That way we all can do better.

For many years autism was a subject that languished in the obscurity of medical and psychiatric journals, but by the winter of 2003 several books had come out that were aimed at a lay audience. I would soon find out that not all of them were right about everything, but the writers were doing what they could. This was a field where the number of cases was increasing exponentially, and with every new case people were learning more. The books were steps in the race.

I had to learn everything I could as fast as I could. It was late March. My doctor's appointment wasn't until April 22nd, and EI was just getting started. Whatever the answer was, I knew that my family and I would have to be active parts of it. A baby can't cure himself.

The more I read the more certain I was: Anthony suffered from autism. As I turned the pages of books, I saw the pattern of Anthony's first fifteen months clearly. One day I sat reading a theory about the role antibiotics play in autism. There on the page I saw my son. I remembered giving him prescriptions: antibiotics for one ear infection after another. Again his cough echoed through my head: more antibiotics. There I was, standing at the pharmacy counter, getting one bottle after another. And now here it was: Anthony's story, in black and white.

It made sense. The antibiotics kill all bacteria – both good and bad in the gut. With no bacteria at all, there is nothing to check the growth of yeast. Good bacteria tries to build up again but the yeast overpowers it. Another bad bug gets in. That causes another infection—more antibiotics, more yeast, weaker immune system and another ear infection. The cycle was more of a downward spiral. I dropped the book and fell to my knees, sobbing.

When I got enough control to punch her number I called my cousin, Kimmy, "I did this to him, Kimmy!" I cried.

"What? You did what?" she asked.

"I did it. I bought them, brought them home, and poured them into the spoon. Spoonful after spoonful I fed him that stuff."

"What stuff? What are you talking about?"

"The antibiotics. Kimmy, I know they're medicine, but they can be toxic too. Every time I got the teaspoon I was feeding my son poison! He opened his little mouth wide and trusted his mom. What did I do to him?"

"Chris, you did what they told you to do, what you had to do. He was hurting. You had no choice."

"I should have taken Daniella out of preschool, or moved someplace warm where he wouldn't get colds… something!"

"Calm down," she said. "There's no way you could know. We all have to make the best decisions we can, and usually that means following doctor's orders. Sometimes that backfires, and we have to try something different. That's what you're doing, isn't it?"

"What?"

"Something different?"

I thought for a moment. "I have to. I have to do everything differently from now on. I have to heal my son."

"I know," she said, "and you will."

I wished I had her confidence. Right at that moment I felt as if I'd spoon-fed my son with a formula for a life of silent darkness.

Later that weekend my cousins came over. They took me to dinner and we had a few drinks. Like Kimmy, they listened to my venting, then they said similar words. It wasn't so much the words, as the comfort they gave me. I needed the encouragement, and God knows I needed to know that they cared.

Once I'd leveled out from the emotional punch of my research, I focused. I was beginning to get a sense of what I might try to help my son. The course that made the most sense to me was in biomedical therapies. These were supposed to help any autistic child, but they made particular sense for Anthony. In my reading I came across an idea that had gained credence in the last decade: many cases of autism weren't there at birth. Instead, these children began developing normally, but regressed. Such a child might recover some of the ground he or she had lost. It was even possible for some children to recover to the point of being diagnosed as autism-free.

Biomedical therapies seemed to be effective in helping these children. These therapies begin with diet and certain supplements. They are based on the child's need for certain vitamins, minerals, probiotics and anti-fungal treatments. Methylcobalomin B-12 shots and chelation are two examples. I read about a number of autistic children who suffered from chronic respiratory and ear infections. Anthony had both. These children had a biochemical disorder linked to an inability to detoxify their bodies of toxins and heavy metals.

Jacqulyn McCandless (DAN doctor, and grandmother of an autistic child) wrote in her book "Children with Starving Brains" that autistic children have a poor immune system, poor digestion, and poor absorption of nutrients. That corresponded to everything I'd seen in Anthony. What really stuck out were the bowel issues these children had, such as diarrhea and constipation. Anthony was still having severe problems with his bowels. As I read Dr. McCandless's book I knew deep down that a large part of Anthony's problem must lie in a weakened immune system. Had it been weakened by antibiotics and vaccines? Probably. Whatever had caused it, the evidence was there: every cold he had turned into a nasty ear infection followed by an asthma attack.

My first experiments with therapies based on diet came from the first book I'd read on autism, "Facing Autism" by Lynn Hamilton. I'd found it completely by accident. I'd wandered into a bookstore to find a children's book. I stood there perusing Seuss, Sendak and all the rest, when my eyes fell upon a volume that was obviously misplaced. From its cover I could tell it was health-related, then I read the title. I picked it up, and was returning it to its proper shelf when I glanced through the contents and introduction. Suddenly it was as if the book was staring at me. "I need this," I thought, and I bought it.

"Facing Autism" guided me through each intervention. Though, like any book on autism, it was limited by the research available at the time it came out, Hamilton's writing made me feel positive. Every page of the book seemed to say: "Begin!" When I reached the part about a gluten-free/casein-free diet I decided to start there. The diet simply made sense to me.

If you are a parent and you suspect your child might be a victim of autism in any of its forms, there are approaches you can try right away. The simplest, easiest one involves cutting out dairy products. There are plenty of substitutes for cow's milk and cheeses. Almond milk is a good alternative to cow's milk. If you take out all dairy products and see a change in your child then you know something is going on, and further action makes sense. This is a single step that often can act as a litmus test. If your child's perception and attention seem to improve right away, keep the child off dairy, and examine what other actions you should take. I will talk later about a diet called the Specific Carbohydrate Diet (SCD). It is far more comprehensive, and helps many autistic children.

In Hamilton's, and in McCandless's books, I learned more and more about a variety of approaches. In diet the main idea was that autistic children had problems breaking down certain strings of amino acids called peptides. In most kids these peptides get flushed out in the urine, but in some children they seep through permeable places in the walls of the intestines and get into the bloodstream.

The theory behind the gluten-free/casein-free diet is this: these peptides come from gluten and casein. This isn't just dairy products and wheat; corn and soy are culprits as well. Some children lack the enzymes to break down some peptides.

The digestive tract is full of enzymes from your intestines all the way up to the saliva in your mouth. You may have seen the processes of enzymes in a baby's body. Have you ever fed your infant some baby food straight from the jar? If you put the partially full jar back in the refrigerator, then take it out the next day it's watery. That's because a little of your baby's saliva got into the food from the spoon you were using. The enzymes from the saliva broke down some of the food and made it watery. If you do this, and the food becomes watery, that doesn't mean your child is free of autism. Autistic children have enzymes. They just don't have enough of the right ones.

This idea of "leaky gut syndrome" made sense to me. Anthony had been having constipation problems for months, which showed me that something must be wrong in his stomach or intestines. Babies with healthy intestinal tracts wouldn't have so many problems with constipation. The wall of their intestine is not worn or permeable to any extent that is troublesome. Once things get there they are supposed to go out. Large amounts of peptides don't leak out.

But if the enzymes aren't there to do the job, the peptides get into the intestinal walls and break through. These peptides that escape into the bloodstream have "opioid" effects. The word "opioid" comes from the same root as "opium" and "opiates." Some of these travel to the brain. There they live up to their name. The numbing effects of opioids are similar to those of narcotics. When I went to hear dietary lecturer Charlie Fall she started describing a disorder. She named a list of symptoms: "Hyperactivity, night wakening, unusually high pain threshold, spaciness, squirminess, sensitivity to sounds, and lack of eye contact. What disorder is it?" "Autism!" we yelled. "No," she said, then she held up a pamphlet, displaying the cover and title. "Those are described in here. For those of you who can't see it, it's called 'Symptoms of a Heroin Addict!' That's what opioids can do—the same effects as heroin, morphine or opium."

Studies have found that autistic children have large quantities of these peptides in their urine. They're called gluteomorphin and caseomorphin, names with the same derivation as morphine. If you have ever taken a narcotic—even codeine for dental pain—you have an idea of what such chemicals can do to the body and brain. Imagine a continuous supply being fed into the developing brain of a baby. I was given a narcotizing drug during Daniella's birth. As it took me under I still had some idea of what was going on, but everything felt foggy and bizarre. I had lost the will to care. It was as if I had lost myself. How will this be in a baby who is just forming? How would a child know that its perception of the world was fading?

As I read about the opioid effect I felt sick. Once again, I felt as if I had spent the last year-and-a-half poisoning my son. I ransacked my kitchen, throwing out anything that had gluten or casein. It was almost everything I was feeding him! When I was done the shelves had so many gaping holes. The refrigerator looked as if it needed refilling. I don't recommend this approach.

Still, eliminating gluten and casein is an important first step in helping an autistic child. In most cases the effects will be sure and relatively quick. If you haven't done anything up to now, you should see the child's attention improve within weeks or even days. You don't have to tear up your kitchen. Just go through each meal and find substitutes. Once you have committed, it needs to be 100% in order to see if the diet is effective. (See Chapter Observations).

I started this diet on a Wednesday. In the last days before I started it I had felt that Anthony was slipping completely away. He had stopped doing even the few things he'd done before—the games that had given me brief glimpses into his closing mind. Up to then he had played peek-a-boo, and clapped his hands to patty cake. If I asked "Where's Mommy's eye?" he pointed at my eye. My favorite was "Give Me a Kiss." But now there were no more kisses.

"Look," I would say to Don. "He's ignoring me. It's like he doesn't know or care that I'm here."

"It looks as though he just doesn't want to be bothered right now," Don said.

"This isn't just right now," I said. "This is every time."

Anthony had done these things before! My memories of those kisses were clearer than any home video. Don knew I was right, but he didn't know what to do either.

Then, early one week we started him on the gluten-free/casein-free diet. The next Sunday morning Anthony awoke in a good mood.

"Give me a kiss," I said tentatively. Anthony turned and planted a kiss directly on my face. "Give me a kiss," I said. He kissed me again. I called for my husband.

"Watch this" I said. "Anthony, give me a kiss." Anthony puckered up and kissed me yet again! "Did you see that?" I shouted. "You try, Don."

Don took Anthony. "Give me a kiss," he said. Anthony smacked his father.

"It's working," I said. "That diet is working."

"It is," Don agreed.

Here is my entry from my diary that day: "April 10, 2003-- We took Ant off the gluten and casein products about three days ago. He has been very alert and he even kissed me on command. He hasn't done that in three weeks. He kissed me every time I asked. His eyes are so bright and alert. He is clapping his hands a lot today. Don said that Anthony went to the art table today and spontaneously was trying to color. He has never done that before."

CHAPTER OBSERVATIONS

Leaky Gut Syndrome

Gluten is a protein found in grains and grain products. Wheat, barely, oats, bulgur, spelt, durum, rye, semolina, couscous, and malt all have gluten. For that reason it is in most bread, cereal, and in many crackers, cookies and other foods. Casein is a protein found in dairy products. Milk, cream, ice cream, cheeses, sour cream, yogurt, and cottage cheese all have it. Both of these proteins are made up of long chains of amino acids. Most of us break down these long chains into single strands so our bodies can properly absorb it for nutritional use.

Picture these proteins as necklaces strung from links (amino acids). The enzymes in your saliva, stomach and intestine work to break these necklaces into single links. If your digestive enzymes don't separate every link, and some strands of links remain, these are peptides. A peptide is a necklace that was only broken down into the size of a bracelet—it still contains several links. Studies have demonstrated that autistic children have more peptides in their urine then typical children.

When there are too many peptides some penetrate the more permeable spots in the walls of the intestine and seep into the bloodstream. This is "leaky gut syndrome." It is similar to having a worn sock. The whole sock represents the intestine. The heel is worn thin, almost translucent, but there is no obvious hole. This is where the peptides leak through. A study conducted by P.D.Eufemia called

"Abnormal Intestinal Permeability in Children with Autism," in *Acta Paediatrica* 85(1996):1076, found that 43% of autistic patients had altered intestinal permeability (leaky gut), and 0% of the 40 controls had leaky gut. (For more information on this see the books "Facing Autism" by Lynn Hamilton, and "Special Diets for Special Kids" by Lisa Lewis.)

Dietary Approaches

You can replace that milk that your child loves with almond milk. For a great almond milk recipe go to www.pecanbread.com. You may worry that your child won't drink almond milk, but if you wean a child slowly (just as you would when you wean them off of formula) they will be accepting. Try adding a little almond milk to a full cup of regular milk. Each day add more almond milk to less regular milk. Within a week or so you can completely eliminate the regular milk. If your child isn't crazy about milk you may not need a replacement. Calcium can be found in plenty of other foods such as Tropicana OJ, vegetables, almonds, walnuts, peanuts, and sunflower seeds. You can get a calcium supplement from www.kirkmanlabs.com. Protein is in all kinds of things from nuts to meats to fish to eggs.

If you see changes in the first weeks then you know you are on the right path. Once you've taken out cow's milk, eliminate all casein products. That means any dairy food: yogurt, cheese, etc. Then you can work on Gluten products. Health food stores abound in this kind of stuff. Here are some of the foods Anthony ate during this time: For breakfast: GFCF (gluten-free/casein-free) waffles, pancakes, sausage, scrambled eggs, and cereal. These products were made with rice, tapioca, and potato. For lunch Anthony would eat hotdogs (Sabrett was our choice if in a pinch). Typically we found some from the health food store without any fillers such as corn. Also you should only buy hot dogs without the nitrates (read labels carefully). I would make homemade chicken nuggets, homemade pizza and leftover dinners. For dinner I would give Anthony chicken, beef, pork, (grilled, roasted, or fried) French fries, vegetables, meatloaf, rice pasta, potatoes and homemade marinara sauce with meatballs.

I found many recipes in the book called "Special Diets for Special Kids" by Lisa Lewis. I also read a helpful book by Karyn Serousi called "Unraveling the Mystery of Autism and Pervasive Developmental Disorders." These two authors created a network called ANDI (Autism Network for Dietary Intervention). Their website, www.autismndi.com, offers a lot of information on the gluten-free/casein-free diet. I have found that people who didn't see results through dietary intervention had foods in the child's diet that had gluten and casein in them. Read labels very carefully. Call the company if you're not sure. This is a big commitment but it needs to be 100%. The pay off is well worth the effort.

Many children have sensitivity to different foods even if they are gluten or casein free. Many autistic children can be sensitive to foods that are high in Phenols. Phenols are chemicals found in all foods. Some foods are very high in Phenols and the body can have trouble processing them. One group of Phenols is called Salicylate. They can be toxic to some children who do not have the enzymes to properly break them down. Salicylates are highly acidic. You may have to rotate the child's diet to see what foods have a negative effect. It may be helpful to eliminate the foods from your child's diet that are high in Phenols. Some symptoms of an adverse reaction to Phenols are dark circles under the eyes, red ears or face, hyperactivity, headaches, aggression, and difficulty sleeping. The foods that are high in Phenols are tomatoes, bananas, apples, red grapes, colored fruits, food dyes, peanuts, milk, and cocoa. A great website that has more information on Phenols is www.danasview.net

Recently there has been research on oxalates and its effects on children with autism. Susan Owens is well known for her knowledge with sulphation. She is a part of the DAN think tank and has begun a study of the Low Oxalate Diet and oxalate dumping. Oxalates are a simple molecule that bind with calcium and then crystallize under certain conditions. The crystals that form can be irritating to tissues causing inflammation. Oxalates come from food and can form. The gut typically won't absorb much of the oxalates and the flora in the gut will metabolize it. If too many oxalates are absorbed, the result is high levels of oxalates in the blood and urine. This is called urine hyperoxaluria. Your body also makes oxalates with could produce high levels in the body. Microbes in the gut eat the oxalates especially lactobacillus acidophilus. However, if the oxalates are in excess they can kill off these good bacteria. Scientists are looking at if this could be why so many children with autism have trouble colonizing the good bacteria. Oxalates help us manage calcium. However, when the body is low in glutathione it can have trouble regulating oxalates. Oxalates can add to oxidative stress which many autistic children have. Dr. Solomons and the foundation working with him found that high oxalates were associating with conditions like vulvodynia, prostatitis, irritable bowel syndrome, fibromyalgia, interstitial cystitis, and skin sensitivity. These conditions improved on the low oxalate diet and with other natural treatments they developed that were found to reduce oxalates. The diet consists of foods that are low in oxalates. I have not tried this with Anthony but have heard positive feedback from parents. I know of parents who are doing SCD diet and trying to keep the foods they feed their child low in oxalates as well. For more information, Susan Owens started a yahoo group called Trying Low Oxalates. For a list of low oxalate foods go to http://www.branwen.com/rowan/index.html (Rowans Resources website)

CHAPTER FOUR

Once I had learned about leaky gut syndrome, and about the problems of too much yeast (see Chapter One, Chapter Observations) I went to the health food store to buy antifungal products. As I was shopping I started talking with the store's owner. When I started telling her about Anthony she became animated.

"I have several customers with autistic children," she said. "From what they tell me it's not as hopeless as it once seemed."

"Have any of them talked about yeast in the gut?" I asked.

"Oh, yes, and what they're learning goes along with what you've been telling me. They think it's all linked: the antibiotics, vaccines, yeast and autism."

"What do they say?" I asked.

"One has autistic twins—both have it," she said.

"I've heard that's not uncommon," I told her.

"Anyway, the doctors told this woman that her twins would probably end up institutionalized. She decided to try to do something, and did anti-yeast treatments along with probiotics—those are the good bacteria like acidopholous. She switched them to gluten-free/casein-free diet. They call it 'GFCF'."

"I'm thinking of trying that," I said. "Has she gotten any results?"

"Very much so. One of her boys is mainstreamed and his twin brother is getting some wonderful results as well. I've got her name and number if you want. She's ready to help anyone with autistic children. She helped another customer of mine. They met right here in the store."

"I'd love to talk to her," I said, and she got me the woman's contact information.

I would come to learn that this is often the way it works in the autism community. We frequent the same stores, lectures, and so on, and we all begin to talk. We have friends among the owners of health food stores, book stores and other related fields, and they introduce us.

These two moms, who had met in the health food store, had also found a lawyer who is father to an autistic child. The lawyer talks on the radio about autism. Together these three parents had just been on a radio program focused on antibiotics and its role in autism.

As I was driving home from the store I was so excited I wanted to blow! This made all the information I was reading a reality for me. Other people—real parents who I would soon meet and talk to—knew about these theories. They were trying these approaches, and even seeing results.

The importance of this lies in the fact that I had yet to talk to any doctors or other professional caregivers who had bothered with such basics as diet. It makes so much sense that the state of one's body would depend on what one puts in it. This would seem to be even more important in a baby who is just forming the structures of organs that are supposed to last a lifetime. Yet the few times I had asked questions relating to what Anthony ate I'd been made to feel that this wasn't much of a concern. Anthony's pediatrician, ENTs, and pulmonologists had looked at me like I had two heads! My only support had come from family and friends.

Now I was finding intelligent, experience-based literature that took diet seriously. And I was about to talk to parents with first-hand experience who had seen recovery. For months the prognoses forming around Anthony had been falling further and further into the shadows. Here were faint, but real rays of light. Children could improve. A child might even recover!

After my conversation at the health food store it dawned on me that Anthony's regressions and improvements corresponded with his changes in diet. We'd changed him to soy formula when he was about eight months old because of his ear infections. Without cow's milk he became less squirmy in my arms. He'd also started smiling, and made better eye contact. At eleven months we'd brought back regular milk in his soy formula to prepare him for weaning off his bottle. In the following months he'd begun losing eye contact. Was it because of cow's milk that he'd become squirmy and irritable again? The idea made sense. This was also when he'd started to only want to watch TV, ignoring our attempts to engage him. Other problems followed the cow's milk. Severe constipation was just one.'

When I'd decided to take Anthony off the formula milk mixture, and put him on only milk without formula I'd gone straight to rice milk. This marked another change. On rice milk Anthony began to let us hold him again. His stiffness and squirminess receded. He even rested his head on my shoulder. My mother had noticed when she babysat. "Anthony actually let me hold him and fell asleep on me," she'd said. This was all making sense now. What I had learned coalesced into a personal epiphany as I drove home from the health food store.

I soon called the mother of the twins. She referred me to a holistic pediatrician.

"She knows her stuff about the biomedical therapies for autism. Call her, and keep doing what you're doing. Follow your instincts, and learn as much as you can."

I told her all about Anthony's infections, and the antibiotics.

"Oh, I know," she said. "My twins had thirty ear infections by the time they were three. I'm a firm believer that antibiotic overuse has something to do with autism. I only wish I'd started on the biomedical cures earlier. I was just like you, doing what the doctors and therapists told me."

She recommended the book "Biomedical Treatments for Autism and PDD" by Dr. William Shaw. She also suggested getting the book I've mentioned, "Special Diets for Special Kids" by Lisa Lewis. I made an appointment with Dr. M (a holistic pediatrician) and ordered the books. I would read each book with my highlighter handy. I still refer to both books constantly.

My path had gone from a book, to a health food store. That led to talking with a mother of autistic twins—a woman who was fighting the battle, and even winning. It was enough to inspire me. The lesson is: Don't try to do this alone. As you travel this path, ask questions. If people start talking to you, listen. If someone hands you a phone number, call it. Pay attention when someone says their children are progressing. Find out details, and see if they fit. Maybe it will be a method you've already tried. Maybe for you it was a dead end. But many times you'll hear of things that work. Some of what you hear might not make sense now, but some aspect of it will fall into place later. Reach out to these other parents. I have learned the most this way. It can shorten your learning curve on issues ranging from biomedical approaches to early education to school district rights. Even when you don't learn anything specific you may give the other parent valuable information.

***

EI told me Anthony would require Applied Behavior Analysis therapy or ABA. ABA is an intensive method where therapists teach skills to autistic children through repetitive demonstration, imitation and performance.

Anthony's first therapist was a woman named Stacy. Stacy remained passive and soft spoken with Anthony, but it didn't matter; he just screamed. She tried to show me how she would teach him to point, but as Anthony's screams continued the whole session seemed fruitless. The second session didn't go much better. It came on April 11th, the day after I had noted in my diary about Anthony's progress on his new diet. My diary entry for April 11th was far less upbeat: "Anthony is having his second ABA therapy session. It is awful. He has been screaming for the longest ten minutes ever! I don't even know what to do with myself. I keep pacing in circles so I figured I'd write. This is best for him I hope. He feels like I've abandoned him with a stranger. Poor baby. He has been alert today and really interacting with Daniella."

When the session was over Stacy said: "Please don't worry about the screaming. I know it sounds bad, but he simply has to get used to the therapy. Most children act this way for the first couple of weeks."

"It does sound bad," I said.

"I know it, but once he realizes that it won't do him any good he'll give up. Then we can settle down and really accomplish something."

I accepted this, but I wasn't entirely happy with it. That much misery didn't give me confidence. Still, I knew he had to learn somehow, and I wasn't aware of other approaches, so I took what I could get.

Next came Michelle. She was the programmer of Anthony's Early Intervention team. Michelle was a tough cookie.

"Here," she said. "I have a list of the things you'll need to get for the team. I want to go over it with you."

"Sure," I said, and we started going through the list. She checked off the things quickly, and with each requirement there seemed to be a rule.

"It's all pretty strict," I said.

"Very strict," she agreed. "It's important that you be on the same page we are."

"Then wouldn't it be good if I understood how this works?" I asked.

"The main thing you need to do is to know what's required, and what the rules are," she said.

"But maybe I could learn some of the things that the therapists are doing, and I could do them with him too."

"Look," she said, "the main thing you can do is just be his mom. That's really the best role for you. Doing the therapy might be difficult for you."

She had a point. She started describing the therapy. "We'll be using his high chair. That way we can strap him in for the sessions. It sounds harsh, but he'll come to accept things much more readily this way. Then we'll be able to make progress."

"Do you really have to strap him in?"

"It's the only way we can be sure he's in a position where he can pay attention," she said. "The sessions are two hours long. If he's not forced to be there with us he won't be."

"Two hours is a long time," I said.

"Long, but necessary."

I took a deep breath, and allowed myself to trust her. It was like the Great Leap of Faith, and I desperately wanted to keep one foot firmly on the ledge. But what could I do? At this point I was just beginning to learn, and I was deeply aware of my dependence on experts.

Michelle had said I should just be his mom, but this didn't stop me from reading. I read all the books on ABA therapy that I could get my hands on. One mother wrote of how much she'd been able to help her two autistic children using ABA. The book was inspiring, but these therapy trials reminded me of dog training.

They ran several trials with Anthony each session. They would make a demand such as "clap your hands" or "point" or "touch your head." They would make the demand ten times in a row. He would be scored according to if he did or did not fulfill it. If Anthony "touched his head" when asked then he would get a piece of cookie, or some other reward. If he didn't respond they would "hand over hand" prompt him to touch his head, then reward him.

The therapists did "mass trialing" with him. This is when you repeat the same trial several times. Again and again they would repeat: "Touch head... touch head.... touch head..." After doing the same trial ten times in a row they would move to the next one. Again and again: ten trials, and on to the next. The idea is that the repetition would produce performance. Once the child does something 90% of the time three days in a row for two separate therapists than it is considered mastered. At that point the team moves on to a new skill. Once Anthony mastered "touch head" then we would move onto "touch nose." It was a new trial but fell into the same category: "Body Parts Identification."

ABA was the primary behavioral therapy given to autistic children. My pediatrician recommended it, just as the therapists had. On the Internet I found an Applied Behavior Analysis workshop being given by Dr. Vincent Carbone that June. I signed up for it. I couldn't just sit by and "be mom." This was my son's life that was at stake. I had to learn everything I could, and use that knowledge in whatever ways were necessary.

Michelle devised a program of several skills that they would teach Anthony through the mass trialing. The therapists kept data sheets to record Anthony's progress. They would present the question to Anthony. If he responded correctly the therapist would write "+." They recorded incorrect responses in various ways according to the degree that it was off.

Anthony's programs were:
look at me
pointing
waving bye-bye
clap hands
blow me a kiss
put arms up
open mouth
say "ah"
tap table
touch cup
put blocks in bucket
touch head
point to Mommy

These were designed to cover several skills such as oral motor, gross motor, fine motor, receptive, family ID, imitation, labeling, etc. They followed the rules: ten times for each program at each session. So if Anthony had nine programs in his red ABA book, then each therapy session he would be asked for 90 responses.

It didn't go smoothly. Anthony fought them every inch of the way. The therapists seemed intimidated by his youth. One therapist, Susan, was very kind and animated, but even with her Anthony bucked and screamed.

One night after a difficult session Susan called me. "I can't go through another bad session with him," she said.

"Please," I said. "Don't worry. I know he's young, but everyone says this is best. I'm sure he'll adjust soon."

After this call I decided to start working with him myself to speed up the adjustment, but even with me he sobbed hysterically. The minute I took out the red ABA program book Anthony started to cry.

"Stay strong," I kept telling myself. "No matter how much it hurts to see him this way, it's what he needs." I told myself it was simply a matter of giving him tough love.

We had two appointments coming up. On April 22nd was my appointment with the Developmental Pediatrician. The second appointment was with the holistic pediatrician on April 24th. Here is an entry from my diary on April 13th: "Anthony and I were on the deck today and he was so alert and playful. His attention span was so different than usual. I kept showing him how to beep the horn of the car and then asked him to 'beep horn' and he did! He was listening. Usually he doesn't listen to what I say or even try to understand. Okay tonight he was amazing! He was so attentive to Don and me. We noticed a decrease in toe walking, and the hand thing he was doing stopped. Tonight he definitely said 'go, go, go,' and we think he was trying to say 'bye bye'. He would say it after we said it and as we waved he watched our hand and then looked at his hand. He was really observing! He would pick his hand up to his belly area and kind of wiggle his fingers. Don and I both feel it was in response to us waving! I pray to God that this diet is really working."

That is how it was just before Anthony's two big doctor visits: a therapy program that seemed more like a nightmare, but also a little boy who was trying so hard to find his way back into the world.

CHAPTER OBSERVATIONS

"Autism" is a word that entered the language in the first half of the 20th century, but few people heard it until the last couple of decades. A part of the reason for this lies in the spread of autism itself. It is becoming more and more obvious that up until the 1990s far fewer children displayed autistic symptoms.

There have always been children with autism. Throughout history people have recorded instances of the severe withdrawal, and totally inward-directed behavior that we now associate with autism. The word was first used by the Swiss psychiatrist, Ernest Bleuler in an article he wrote in 1912. It comes from the ancient Greek word αὠτοσ, meaning "self." Bleuler was writing about schizophrenics, but the word was revived in the 1940s by Dr. Leo Kanner at Johns Hopkins Hospital. Kanner was the first to describe a set of observed symptoms, and label them as the condition "autism." A similar, but less severe set of symptoms was classified as Asperger's Syndrome by Lorna Wing in her 1981 medical paper. She named the syndrome after Austrian psychiatrist and pediatrician, Dr. Hans Asperger

These two definitions have remained at the core of diagnoses of autism to this day, but ideas about causes and treatments for autism have changed greatly. At any moment many different people will tell you many different things about why children are autistic, and you will hear just as many ideas about what should be done about it. One of the "problems" is that so many solutions are being found. Some are more effective than others, and there are those that work better in certain circumstances. In her book about autism Dr. Jacquelyn McCandless writes in regard to her own autistic granddaughter: "I will continue to remain open to new discoveries sure to come in this rapidly evolving field, while loving [Chelsey] with all my heart however she grows." This kind of openness and love must lie at the core of any successful therapy for an autistic child.

As I have already noted, at this writing (Spring, 2006) more and more parents and professionals are convinced that many cases of autism that have been diagnosed in the last fifteen years have been caused, wholly or partially, by mercury that has been used in many vaccines for infants, and by an overuse of antibiotics in the first year of life. Some also feel that the front-loaded schedule of vaccines (so many in the first year and a half of life) contributes to the increase.

These notions stem from the idea that autistic symptoms are related to disorders in the immune system. Mercury can devastate the immune system. Vaccines and antibiotics are taxing on it too. This is even truer in children, and particularly in infants.

However, if these ideas are right, it also means that many of the children who are being diagnosed with autistic disorders have a fighting chance at partial and even full recovery. This may not be true of every autistic child, but it is possible that the vast majority can improve a great deal. The most important steps come in detoxifying the child's system, and feeding them diets that promote healing.

***

Therapies for autism began with O.I. Lovaas in the 1960s. At that time he did research with autistic children using Discrete Trial Training. This is the protocol that Early Intervention agencies use (the mass trials I described earlier). In this therapy there are several programs teaching different skills. Together these fall under the heading of Applied Behavior Analysis (ABA) therapy.

Later on I will describe Verbal Behavior (VB) techniques that have been developed since the time of Lovaas. VB has its roots in the work of behaviorist, B.F. Skinner.

CHAPTER FIVE

On the day of our appointment with the developmental pediatrician, Don was away on business. I went to work worried.

"I know we already have a preliminary diagnosis," I told my friends Mary and Michelle, "but I still feel funny going in there."

"Maybe it's just because you don't want to hear a diagnosis," said Mary.

"Maybe."

"Or you don't want to think of a diagnosis as being complete... could that be it?" Michelle asked.

"Yeah, something like that," I said. "When I read these books, and talk to the other people who have autistic kids, I feel hope, but whenever I talk to all the medical professionals—the doctors and therapists—they make me feel like we just have to make the best of this terrible situation. I don't want to think like that."

"Then don't," said Michelle.

"That's right... don't give in to that kind of thinking," Mary agreed. "Just listen for whatever there is that's positive... the things you can do to beat this. Don't worry if they tell you that 'leave it to us' stuff. Just listen for whatever makes sense in helping Anthony, and fit that in with what you're doing."

"But I don't even know what I'm doing," I said.

"Okay, but you're going to figure it out," said Mary.

Michelle nodded. "You will."

As I left I broke down. They both gave me big hugs. "Stay strong," they said.

As I was driving home to pick up Anthony for the appointment, I called my mom. I was crying. I didn't want to face any of it. I just wanted to scratch this day off my calendar. Mom got my father to meet me at the pediatrician's office.

Her office was at the hospital where Anthony had been born. Just pulling into the parking lot depressed me further. We had left this place with such hope seventeen months earlier. Now the place seemed like an eerie ghost of those hopes.

My father was there, and he sat with us as I filled out a ton of paperwork. My hand was shaking as I wrote. I felt nauseous.

The developmental pediatrician (we'll call her Dr. S.) called us in. Though her office wasn't so different from any doctor's office, I felt threatened. To me the toys seemed old, their edges a little worn and fraying. I think she sensed my fears.

"Don't worry," she said. "We're going to do all we can. I'm not saying you should get your hopes up too high, but in most of these cases there are real possibilities for improvement, as long as we follow certain regimens."

I nodded. "Thank you," I said.

Her tone was kind, and she did her best to make it easier. She asked me questions as she tried to stir Anthony's interest with several toys. I could see that these were exercises, and she was watching his reactions carefully. After about an hour she brought us to her office.

"Please wait here," she said. "I'll be right back."

When she returned she held a folder. Something about it, or her manner, or both, rang alarm bells in my mind. Then I realized: this was the diagnosis.

"I've gone over the records," she said, "and with those, and what I see today, I'm diagnosing Anthony with Autism Spectrum Disorder/PDD-NOS."

"I'm sure I've read about that one," I said, "but there are so many of them. Exactly what kind of autism is that?"

"It's one of those types I was telling you about," she said, "the kind that may improve somewhat with the proper therapy. It's even possible that Anthony might progress to something equivalent to a functional stage. It's happened before. But you must understand that there are no panaceas. It's a lifelong disability. To get any improvement will require a lot of work. You've done the right thing, getting in the early intervention providers. Do everything you can to cooperate with them. They know what they're doing."

I sat listening, trying to remember what Michelle and Mary had told me. How do you only listen to the good parts? I had the surreal feeling of being caught in a world that was not my own. I wanted to get out of there. I had known what she was going to say, yet somehow, in that office, with the businesslike feel of the desk, walls, and files, she had all of the authority.

My mind raced. Her voice grew fuzzy in my ears. She was going into detail about this disorder, doing her best to educate me. "You have to understand... the nature of the illness... and the difficulties...emotional toll... trust..." I can recall every movement of her lips, and every time she made eye contact with me, but I cannot remember a single complete sentence of her speech. Her utterances split into phrases, then into words, then into disjointed syllables. Suddenly she sounded like the grownups on the Peanuts shows on TV, the ones you hear from off screen, saying: "Wa, wa, wa, wa, wa..." That was all I heard.

Finally she wound down, and I spoke: "I've been working on his diet," I said. "I took out dairy, and I'm getting him gluten-free and casein-free. As I've been doing it I've seen some big changes in him, all for the good. He pays attention much better than he used to."

"I'm afraid I can't recommend that," she said. "Really what he needs is the same healthy diet you would give any child. When you take something basic out of a child's diet you may be taking out essentials without knowing it. I know you're conscientious, and make substitutions, but you can't be sure you're replacing everything. Dietary approaches to autism have no proven value. The one thing that does work is ABA therapy, and from the record it looks as if you're already on the way with that. I'm glad you are, because ABA really might help. In fact, if he's improving, it's probably because of that."

"But during the sessions all he does is cry," I said. "How can he learn anything if all he does is scream and bawl?"

"That may be all you see, but believe me, it's Anthony's chance at improvement," she said.

I was polite, but as I left I felt my anger building. I knew what I was seeing! Why didn't she believe me? "She's wrong," I told my father. "I'm not sure what the answer is, but I don't think she has it."

"Doctors don't always see everything," he said. "You'll figure it out, Chris. Just listen to her about his general health. That's what the doctors can help with. But for this, you've got to keep doing what you're doing."

"But, Dad, I can't figure out what I'm doing."

"You will."

His attitude was reflective of my friends and family. Over the next couple of days I was flooded with phone calls from them telling me to keep my chin up. They patiently listened to me cry and vent, as I tried to make sense of my thoughts. I knew I was going to see the holistic pediatrician, so I focused on that. I needed every bit of information I could gather to help Anthony.

***

This second doctor's appointment was only two days later, a Thursday. We'll call the holistic pediatrician: Dr. M. I had made this appointment on the advice of the mother of autistic twins, and I looked to Dr. M with hope for some understanding of what I was trying to do. Still, she was a doctor—a medical professional—and so far I hadn't had much luck with them.

Her office was in a large building, but it wasn't big itself. It was a cozy little suite of rooms. Her receptionist was off, and the first thing we heard was Dr. M's voice from the back. "Come in," she called. As I walked through the outer office I saw one wall papered with photos. They were all of kids she had helped. There were thank-you notes that went with the pictures. The little faces looked happy. I felt as if I was in a very different place. I didn't feel the nervousness. Instead I felt as if doors opened more easily here.

Dr. M's manner was blunt, and I got the feeling that her approach was transparent. What you saw was what you got.

"Anthony has been through a lot," she said. "He's damaged and intoxicated."

"Intoxicated?" I asked.

"Yes. I don't mean like he's drunk on alcohol, but there are similarities. All the things we give our infants now—all our medical advances—some of them aren't so advanced. They get into the brain and shut things off, just like alcohol does with someone who's had a few too many."

"So can we sober him up?" I asked.

She laughed. "Oh, I think we can. Anthony seems very promising to me. I think we can bring him a long, long way—maybe all the way—back to normal. He will be a perfect child!"

I told her what I'd done with his diet.

"That's smart," she said. "Biomedical interventions can do so much to save a child like Anthony."

"You really think so?" I asked.

"Of course. The damage came from things we put in his body. We can undo the damage by putting in more healthy things."

"I can't believe you're saying that," I said. "No one else has."

"I know. A lot of doctors don't believe it, but it's what I believe."

Dr. M wanted to boost his immune system and heal his gut. She felt that all the antibiotics had destroyed his immune system and digestive tract. She was appalled at all the medication he has been on for ear infections and asthma. Anthony was taking a very high dose of Flovent twice a day for his asthma. It was a dosage usually prescribed for adults many times his size.

"I want you to go to the health food store and get some things," she said, writing on a pad. "These are boosters for the immune system. Also, I'm prescribing probiotics. Essentially those are the good bacteria in your digestive tract. They fight off yeast and bad bacteria. If he takes them the good bacteria will grow back, and we can put a stopper on that leaky gut."

Two days earlier, after listening to a message of hopelessness, I had walked out of a pediatrician's office close to tears. Today I left Dr. M's ready to face a challenge. I drove straight to the health food store and bought the items she recommended.

After getting Anthony on his supplements to boost his immune system I noticed that he didn't have the same thick mucus always running out of his nose. I was quite certain that taking the dairy away had helped this. I decided to stop his inhalers. I did this on my own, but I don't suggest that you do it without some advice. Talk to your doctor first. Together you can decide if this is right for your child. For us it seemed to work, along with all the other things we were doing. Anthony seemed less spacey, more attentive and much happier. Up until then I had been describing Anthony as either "here," meaning in our world, or "out" meaning disconnected from us. So much of the time I'd had to admit he was "out." Now he was definitely more "here." He seemed more interested. I didn't have to work as hard to engage him. I saw my son truly awake for the first time!

He began to notice Austin and Daniella. As he would watch them play he would start to giggle. He was figuring out there were pets in his life. Before that, for all Anthony cared our dog, Pretty, may as well have been a piece of furniture. Now he realized that she was a living, breathing animal. With all the other problems, I'd barely considered that Anthony didn't interact with Pretty. Now I remembered that Austin and Daniella had always been touching our animals at this age, and finally so was Anthony. At long last, our son was becoming more social.

His therapists noticed too. His sessions went more smoothly, with fewer tears. He still had a long way to go. His therapists worked relentlessly, trying to get him to point. He wouldn't. Though my official instructions were to "just be a mom," I tried to help. I made pointing into a game. I would drop something he wanted and say: "What do you want?" Then I would prompt his finger into a point, grab what he wanted and give it back to him. Over and over I would do this.

With Austin and Daniella I'd always taken pointing for granted. One day those little fingers just stuck out and they were pointing at anything and everything! Were they just pointing at something new, or something they wanted? I never had to think much about that. Usually I just knew. It was nature. Yet with Anthony this seemed to be such a huge bar to learning and growing up. How could he show me what he wanted, or what he was thinking about? How could he identify anything without pointing? This is a stage of learning that most of us don't pay any attention to, yet it stays with us throughout our lives just as surely as speech does. If you think of any moment when you were in visual contact with someone, but, for some reason, couldn't speak out loud, you'll see that pointing is the most basic signal we have.

Dr. M had us back in for some tests. She tested Anthony's hair, and she did an organic acid test. The hair analysis showed some heavy metal but not much, and it didn't reveal any mercury. The organic acid tests showed that Anthony had high levels of yeast and gastrointestinal bacteria.

"There should be more metals. There should be mercury," Dr. M said.

"Why?" I asked.

"We all take in some toxins no matter how pure our food. Some metals we need in low levels, but then they reach the level of toxicity. When we don't need a metal we should be excreting it, sometimes through the hair, other times through sweat, urine, or feces. In some way the excess should make its way out of us. There are theories—and the more I see, the more I think it's a fact—that autistic children don't excrete these things as well as other children. It may settle in their body, and build up. When those metals build up in the brain, that spells trouble."

What Dr. M was saying made sense to me, and as I read further I agreed with her even more. Heavy metals can be found everywhere in our environment. They are particularly prevalent in some things that babies love to put in their mouths. All of us know about the problems with lead paint, and we realize that lead enters a child's system because of what they put in their mouths. A teething child might chew on anything he or she can reach. Lead is something we've learned about, and now it is public policy to protect children from it. Most of us realize mercury causes problems too, but most of us only think of it in terms of fish. We've heard about the mercury in tuna. Because most of us eat a tuna fish sandwich now and then, we think of mercury in regard to ourselves, or even in the sense of how it affects the population as a whole. We seldom consider it in terms of just babies.

But mercury and other heavy metals can be found in batteries. It is also used as preservatives in vaccines, cleaning supplies, pesticides, deodorant, shampoos, over-the-counter nasal sprays, ear and eye drops, anabolic steroids, sunscreen, dental amalgams, hemorrhoid creams and, finally, seafood.

Medicines that help, both in studying this problem, and in treatments, are called chelators. These are medications that act as magnets, pulling heavy metals from the body. Mercury suppresses the immune system and wrecks havoc on the neurological system. It does all this while still inside our bodies. Because this mercury hasn't been expelled, a hair test won't be an indicator of what's still in the body. You need to first give the child a chelator-provoking agent prescribed by your doctor, such as DMSA, then check the blood and urine to see what the level of metals are that your body is excreting. Heavy metals can also affect vitamin utilization, nutritional deficiencies, toxin levels, and digestion.

Anthony was very low in several essential minerals. This is common with autistic children. We ordered a multi-vitamin/mineral supplement. This is designed for children with autism. We also started an anti-fungal treatment by giving Anthony garlic supplements. Garlic is a good anti-bacteria and anti-fungal supplement. It helps to kill off those unwanted bugs. Another good antifungal supplement is grapefruit seed extract. This is very potent so you need to start very slow. We used one drop and worked up to four drops over several weeks. I did both garlic and the extract, but alternated them. You should always alternate anti-fungal treatments.

When starting an antifungal/anti-bacteria treatment there can be a die-off effect, which can bring negative reactions. These can range from mild to severe. Picture the candida (yeast) as bunches of grapes in your gut. As you kill off the grapes they burst, and out flows a toxin. Enough toxins can produce flu-like symptoms. This usually lasts a couple of days but it could be more. As long as these symptoms aren't too severe you shouldn't be alarmed; they show that what you're doing is working.

Still, you want to reduce the negatives as much as possible. Killing off the bad bugs in the gut means that you need to add in the good guys. To do this, start on a good bacteria like probiotics before giving your child an anti-fungal. When you do start the anti-fungal, take it slow. Build up the dosage over the course of two weeks. If you do this you may avoid some of the problems.

Sleep had been a problem for Anthony ever since he was six months old. He was an awful sleeper! Both of our other children had woken up from time to time, but we had always been able to coax them back to sleep. Not Anthony. Even if we brought him to our bed he couldn't lay still long enough to drop off to sleep. I couldn't sit with him and rock him, and if we let him cry than Daniella would wake up. Every night it was a two-hour drill to get him back to sleep. By that time it was almost morning. This constant wakefulness added to our growing exhaustion.

I read that autistic children lack Melatonin. Melatonin is what our body naturally produces when it gets dark outside. It's the signal for our body to sleep. We started giving Anthony a Melatonin supplement a half hour before bedtime. It helped. He still woke up during the night but he fell back to sleep much faster.

CHAPTER OBSERVATIONS

Going to the developmental pediatrician was difficult, but I am not saying there was no use to it. We kept going to traditional pediatricians and to Dr. M. It's best to remember that autism is a field where the medical knowledge is always playing catch-up. Your developmental pediatrician is likely to know all of the accepted therapies, which will also help you find state and county programs for which your child qualifies. Those who practice holistic medicine, and work in other alternative fields, are more likely to know what's being tried out on the cutting edge. Some of that knowledge will be just a step away from general medical acceptance. Other ideas will be more experimental.

Going to both kinds of doctors will give you more information. Just as important, it will expose you to different points of view. Those who experiment almost always have hope, and in the early stages you need that badly. With any medical advice it's always good to be careful. Listen to your common sense. When dealing with the mystery of autism, and with the medical response to it, it's best to recall words written by the world's most famous pediatrician sixty years ago: "You know more than you think you do." Dr. Spock opened his book with those words, and they are still true today. A great deal of a parent's knowledge lies in intuition and common sense. Get all the information you can, then look carefully at your child, and make your decisions.

***

Among the early tests that Dr. M ran was an organic acid test from Great Plains Laboratory. This was the test that revealed high levels of yeast and gastrointestinal bacteria. Their website is www.greatplainslaboratory.com.

At this point we were also starting Anthony on a calcium supplement. There are several of these, and they may be coming up with new ones. We ordered this through Kirkman Laboratories, which has an excellent website to keep you up to date at www.kirkmanlabs.com.

In a recent study from the *International Journal of Toxicology*, when the hairs from autistic children's first baby haircuts were compared to those of typical children the children with autism showed little or no mercury, while the normal children's results had higher mercury levels. As

Dr. M mentioned, the body excretes toxins such as mercury through hair, sweat, urine, and feces. A typical child's body gets rid of the mercury through the hair, detoxifying properly. The child with Autism doesn't. The mercury then builds up to dangerous neurotoxin levels. (A.S. Holmes, M.F. Baxill, and B.E. Haley in the *International Journal of Toxicology,* 2003; 22:277-285.)

With the problems we've had with fish we should realize that mercury is one of the most poisonous substances on the planet. It has no business being anywhere near our children in vaccines or anything else. Mercury poisoning affects the immune system, the gastrointestinal tract, and the neurological system—the problem areas of autistic children.

In July, 2000 Dr.Stephanie Cave testified to the Congressional Committee on Government Reform: "I believe that the introduction of the Hepatitis B [HIB] vaccine in 1991 has sparked this recent [autism] epidemic. Because of HIB, the exposure to mercury exceeds the EPA safe limits for the metal... The EPA safe limits are usually related to ingested mercury, which is partially cleared by the liver... The two-month dose of mercury is at least 30 times higher than the recommended daily maximum exposure as set by the EPA."

She went on to cite an article in the *Journal of Pediatrics,* 2000 where two researchers named Stajeck and Lopez compared mercury in the blood of infants at birth, prior to the Hepatitis B injections, and after. Mercury levels rose in the blood of the infants tested. In some preterm infants there were levels that measured ten times that seen in term infants. Dr. Cave noted that bile production is minimal in infants, making it more difficult for metals to be cleared from the body. When added to a vaccine, the metals are even more dangerous because the vaccines trigger immune reactions that may increase the permeability of the gastrointestinal tract. When it reaches the brain mercury affects precisely the sections affected in autism.

According to an article in *Journal of American Physicians & Surgeons* 2003; 8:76-79, "A Case-Control Study of Mercury Burden in Children with Autistic Spectrum Disorders" by J. Bradstreet, D.A. Geier, J.J. Kartzinel, J.B. Adams, and M.R. Geier: "Emerging epidemiologic evidence and biologic plausibility suggest an association between autistic spectrum disorders and mercury exposure. This study compares mercury excretion after a three-day treatment with an oral chelating agent in children with autistic spectrum disorders and a matched control population. Overall, urinary mercury concentrations were significantly higher in 221 children with autistic spectrum disorders than in eighteen normal controls. Regardless of the mechanism by which children with autistic spectrum disorders have high urinary mercury concentrations, the DMSA treatment described in this study might be useful to diagnose their present burden of mercury."

In other words, the signs definitely point to mercury as the culprit.

CHAPTER SIX

Anthony's health was improving. This alone seemed like a huge accomplishment, especially in the face of some of the more traditional medical predictions. His runny nose had finally dried up, and he was more resistant to colds. When he did catch cold it wasn't an automatic threat of major illness. The severe fevers, ear infections and asthma attacks were mostly things of the past. This meant that he didn't need the antibiotics. Finally the vicious cycles were being replaced by more healthful patterns.

Even his bowels were more regular. They weren't perfect. He still didn't have formed stools. One day it would be like clay and the next it was like mud. Still, I was happy that he could have a bowel movement without the need of an enema, or me taking his rectal temperature. Those little things mount up into big changes. Our lives were getting better.

I told all this to his pediatrician, pulmonologist and E.N.T.—the regular medical professionals. They didn't express any displeasure at the progress, but they were sure I was wrong about the cause.

"It's all well and good," said one, "but I would hesitate to give credit to any of those diets you have him on. Diet is important, but all he really needs is meals that supply the basic nutrition any child needs. It's the ABA therapy that will help him, and I'm sure that's working, and making a big difference in your life."

"But the stool, the sleeping, the runny nose... all those are better," I said. "Don't you think this kind of diet might help other kids?"

She shook her head. "It's the therapy. They're coming up with great new approaches all the time. Your ABA therapists are doing an excellent job. I think that's what you're seeing here."

"But how can their pointing at things change his bowel movements?"

"It's the whole approach," she said.

"But he's still not learning how to point. It's all the other stuff that's getting better."

"Don't worry," she said. "It all fits. Just be mom, and I'm sure we can help Anthony a lot."

I would run up against this again and again: conventional medicine is not open to natural approaches. It is a viewpoint that infuriates any parent who wants to see the whole picture. A conventional pediatrician should have information about any safe treatments that might help, but instead they warn parents against them. They put out these warnings without doing their own research. It's true that doctors should be careful, but that notion translates into an attitude of: "If I don't know about it, it must be damaging."

The parent of an autistic child will find two distinct worlds: conventional medicine and holistic medicine. The two should compliment one another, but instead they are set up in opposition, like boxers in the corners of a ring. It leaves it up to us parents to referee the boxing match, and see who wins each round.

My journal entry from Mothers Day, 2003 goes like this: "How different Anthony has been the last two weeks. He is truly alert and playful. He is initiating play with the kids. He keeps watching the dogs and cat. Before the animals and his siblings might as well have been furniture in the room. Anthony never noticed them. He is so amazing socially. We can see a huge difference in him. As if he is awake for the first time. He is truly aware of his surroundings. Yesterday, he was at a party and he was laughing while he watched all the kids playing. We are so hopeful that the biomedical therapy is helping him!" This was just a few weeks after our first concerted efforts with diet, supplements, and vitamins.

Around this time I started going to a support group with other parents of autistic children. This is something I strongly suggest to others. While family and friends are supportive, and nothing can replace their love, you also need to talk to others who are in your exact predicament. These parents are fighting the same battle you are. When they hear about diets, supplements, ABA, and all the rest, it's not a foreign language. It's the world they are living in too. Families are built to give sympathy. They are great at calming the nerves in a tough moment, but in the day-to-day struggle they don't always pick up on every nuance, or on the big picture. In your less confident moments you may find yourself wondering if they take your efforts seriously. Sometimes a stray comment can sow such doubts. A relative talks to a medical friend, and hears nothing but negative words about alternative treatments. Immediately that relative's support becomes purely emotional, while the "sensible" part of them is shaking its head.

With other parents of autistic kids you can speak freely, listen, and debate the merits of any new approach, using your own experience and theirs as the true yardstick for success. You can swap ideas and talk about different treatments saying whether they were a waste of time or helpful. With other parents you know that your experience counts. You are all there, searching together. I have learned more about autism from other parents than from any other resource. Through our own trial and error we can help one another.

It was when Anthony was a year-and-a-half that I began to realize that I needed to start consciously setting aside time for myself. I had been so consumed by the battle that I hadn't considered the inner resources I needed to fight it. Now I began to see that I need to do something for myself; otherwise I might be headed for a big fall.

Most of it was little things. I went to the gym if I could. Sometimes, if I simply couldn't get away from the house, I would put on a yoga tape for an hour, and follow the techniques. As you go through this I also strongly recommend doing these kinds of things for yourself. Remember, it's *you* who has to deal with this crisis day after day. To do that you have to stay in shape both mentally and physically.

Make sure you have some moments of relaxation, and don't feel guilty about them. Yes, you do need time away from your child, and it should be guilt-free. This is doubly important when you have a needy child. It's easy to wallow in guilt. You'll even find yourself feeling guilty about the wallowing. Don't fall into this trap. If you feel you're getting close to it, don't hesitate to seek counseling. Many mothers need it, and not enough get it.

Go out with friends, see a movie, or go running—anything that helps you blow off excess steam, or level out when things seem too crazy. If you do this, you'll be much better prepared for whatever situation comes up by the time you get home.

You have to avoid hitting the brick wall. It's there, waiting for you to crash into it, and you won't necessarily see it coming. An autistic child needs us at our best, especially in the first months and years. Our families need our best efforts as well. It's a test of our energy, faith, and strength.

This is equally true of fathers. Don would coach sports as a coping mechanism. He loves sports and children. This gave him an opportunity to take his mind off Anthony's autism. Practices and games gave him something to look forward to.

Football took a lot of his time, and Austin's too. Though football is a sport I can do without, I wasn't about to stop them. I knew that they both needed it. It was quite a commitment. Practices were every day, and they played on both Saturday and Sunday.

I tried taking Anthony to practices and games, but it wasn't easy. He had no idea of what was going on. Who knows what a boisterous crowd looks like through the eyes of a little boy whose brain is being choked? He would cry and scream as the people around us cheered. I told the people around us about his sensory difficulties, and most of them understood that he wasn't just another bratty kid. Parents were the most empathetic about this. They asked questions, and I found that I enjoyed answering them, and giving them a crash course on autism. It took my mind off all those other children of ours, crashing into one another out on the field.

At home I had other outlets. We live on a mountain with beautiful views, and plenty of places to walk. Our dog, Sheeba, a huge English Mastiff, is always ready to go out. Sheeba and I would take long walks, and when I got home I would be more ready to deal with whatever came. There is nothing like a 150-pound dog who loves to play. She knew how to give me some of my best breaks from the long battle with autism.

As Anthony passed a year-and-a-half, spring changed into summer. His response to the diets and supplements was more and more encouraging. He was no longer deaf to his name. His health improved markedly. Still, he wasn't talking, and despite all the efforts of his therapists he wasn't pointing.

I wanted to learn more about what I could do for him, so I decided to sign up for a three-day ABA workshop. It was being given at a college in Monmouth County, about two hours from our home, so I decided to stay at my grandmother's house twenty minutes from there. I had a lot of second thoughts. Could I leave the kids for that long? Would Don be able to handle them and Anthony?

Go," Don told me. "If you don't you'll regret it."

"But can you—"

"Don't ask. We can handle things here. You want to learn everything you can, and besides, it'll be good for you to get away."

So I drove to my grandmother's, and the next day I went to the opening session.

When I first got to the college auditorium I was intimidated. I hadn't realized how much this conference was aimed at professionals—doctors, nurses, therapists, and teachers. There were very few parents. Now, three years later, I can see that was how it worked then. Parents were just beginning to figure out that, as active participants in the fight against autism, they had to learn all that they could. Too often they were hearing the same thing I was: "Just be mom." Too often they were following orders. Today most of the participants at such a conference would be parents.

As it was, we were a tiny minority, and I was thankful when I saw a face I knew. It was a woman I'd gone to high school with, Marissa. Marissa didn't have an autistic child. She was there to train in a Verbal Behavior (VB) program that she would be using the following fall. She taught autistic children. Though she was as professional as the rest of them, seeing her helped me feel more at home.

"I'm just here as a mom," I said.

"Then you're in the right place," said Marissa. "A mom is the most important professional in an autistic kid's life. You're the one who faces the problem from morning-to-night. More parents ought to come to these things."

"Do you really think so?" I asked, looking around at all the MDs and PhDs.

"I know so. You'll get a lot out of this. If you've read anything at all you'll understand enough of what's going on."

"Oh, I've been reading," I said.

The featured speaker was Dr.Vincent Carbone. He is a board certified Behavior Analyst with over twenty-five years of experience helping children with autism. He started out explaining the history of Applied Behavior Analysis (ABA).

Dr. Carbone showed how the discoveries about autistic symptoms coincided with research about behavior and the development of therapies. To understand it fully, we need to break from our story, and take a history lesson, one that brought me to an epiphany about how nearly a century of discovery could help heal my son.

CHAPTER SEVEN

This chapter contains information on the therapy I used to help recover my son. Even after a year of discrete trials my son was non verbal and had very little skills. Then we found Verbal Behavior and it taught him to speak spontaneously! It contains a breakdown of what ABA/Verbal Behavior is. It begins by explaining the history of ABA based on BF Skinner's analysis. Hard to make the history part very sexy but press on and you won't be disappointed.

This therapy was one of the most important parts of Anthony's recovery. Its importance can't be stated strongly enough. Please read this chapter carefully. My hope is that you embrace verbal behavior. It truly helped my son—who was nonverbal when I started—find his voice and his way back.

Anyone who has read much about 20th century psychology knows of B.F. Skinner, but the rest of us may not have heard his name. I hadn't.

Skinner was the chief proponent of the behaviorist school of psychological theory. He theorized that many psychological disorders could be improved by conditioning: always reward desired behavior, and withhold rewards for undesirable behavior.

In 1938 Skinner published his first book: "The Behavior of Organisms." In it he reported on his studies of rats. The studies showed that behavior was based on consequences and learning: an organism reacts to whatever it experiences. It reacts favorably to that which gives it nurture or pleasure, and unfavorably to that which doesn't. This would seem like common sense, but it went against the accepted theory that an organism's behavior is determined by its intentions. In this book Skinner was becoming one of the founders of the behaviorist school of psychology. Behaviorism said that we are creatures of experience and consequences.

From this comes the conclusion that we can teach a child by creating conditions where a desired action brings a good consequence. In other words, when they do what we want, we make them happy. This reinforces their behavior, and they then repeat the action without prodding. This is the principle behind Applied Behavior Analysis (ABA).

Skinner followed up with a book called: "Science and Human Behavior" in 1953, then in 1957 he wrote "Verbal Behavior." These books refined his ideas, but attracted only a limited academic audience. In Skinner's book "Verbal Behavior" it demonstrates his ideas that speaking and communicating is based on behavior. To teach verbal behavior you should be a scientist and experiment, not following a recipe. Two years after "Verbal Behavior" was published, in 1959 a professor by the name of Noam

Chomsky published a review of Skinner's "Verbal Behavior" book. Chomsky disagreed with Skinner in his review. Chomsky felt language was innate and embedded in our minds. This started a debate among many in the field. . .

Skinner's theories found their link with autism in the 1960s when O.I. Lovaas of UCLA began using behaviorist theories to treat children with autism. At the time the most prevalent ideas about the origins of the condition centered around the image of a "refrigerator mom." This was rooted in the theory that autistic children got that way because their mothers were cold, and never showed them warmth or love. Lovaas in addition to Bettleheim cast doubt on that, and wondered if autism was more of a learning problem. If it was, then maybe autistic children would react well to behavior modification. He experimented, using the process Skinner had described: antecedent (what happens directly before a behavior occurs), behavior, and consequence (what happens after a behavior occurs). He used discriminative stimuli (SDs). These are signals that a response will be reinforced with a particular result—or, in the case of an autistic child, that a particular object or situation will cause the child to act in a particular way. With these tools Lovaas broke down each skill into simple steps. His idea was that you could teach a child each step, showing the child how one led to the other. As long as children saw each result as desirable they would want to learn the behavior that brought it about.

Up until behaviorists such as Lovaas, doctors who encountered autism held out little hope. Most doctors assumed it was a psychological condition, but they had no effective way to treat it. Pediatricians and general practitioners looked to psychiatrists and psychologists for guidance. These fields were stuck with "refrigerator mom." But if the patient's problem was with mom, what was a shrink to do? Find Mom a thermostat? Get the child to talk about it? Conversations with children deep into autism tend to be pretty one-sided. It was also inconvenient that many of these refrigerator moms seemed like warm, sensitive women who displayed nothing but love for their children. But theories die hard. Though Lovaas's methods met with success they were ignored by many in mainstream psychology.

Lovaas's approach was a step forward, but in my opinion it had problems. For one thing it wasn't particularly adaptable. It asked the child to adjust to each step, the method didn't leave the teacher with much room to alter what he or she was doing. In this sense Lovaas didn't use Skinner's ideas concerning adaptability.

Skinner understood that a teacher would have to change with varying circumstances. Years later a teacher in the field named Doug Grier put it roughly like this: To be a successful teacher you must act like a strategic scientist constantly evaluating the situation and changing yourself according to the child.

This means that a teacher, therapist or researcher must continually be willing to stretch the principles of Applied Behavior Analysis (ABA) to allow for experimentation. Just as the student must adapt to the stimuli presented by the teacher, the teacher must adapt to the student's reactions, seeing if those reactions might indicate a different path to the same goal. This is experimental analysis of behavior. Your interaction with the child should be a dynamic process where you constantly change your tactics depending on the child's behavior. With this method you don't lead the child through a rigid set of instructions in a recipe. You find the instructions and ingredients that work.

A few years after Lovaas started experimenting with the beginnings of ABA, Jack Michael, a behavior analyst, was using Skinner's "Verbal Behavior" as a text for his students at Western Michigan University. He, Mark Sundberg, and Jim Partington began experiments similar to those done by Lovaas.

Starting with Lovaas's method, they added other principles from Skinner's analysis. Recognizing that many autistic children wouldn't respond at all to verbal language, they began with sign language. They started with the simplest sign of all: pointing at something. From this they moved through up the levels to more complex signing, using the universal sign language developed for communication among the deaf. Once they had some language skills established they could develop such tools as mands (requests), tacts (labels), and intraverbal (talking about something not present). They were moving into areas that required more abstract communication involving things beyond the here-and-now. Much of Skinner's analysis of verbal behavior held up with the use of sign language. Once autistic children could grasp the language they could begin to learn behaviors and skills. Sundberg, Michael, and Partington went on to publish articles and dissertations about what they had found. .

It was Lovaas's Applied Behavior Analysis methods, with their discrete trials and mass trials that first took hold among doctors and therapists as the new way of dealing with autism. By the '70s this was finally happening. Lovaas's research had come earlier than that coming out of Western Michigan U, and he had challenged the old theories involving psychological traumas such as refrigerator moms. The group from WMU quietly developed their new therapies, experimenting, adjusting, and training a few other therapists to do the same, but they weren't publishing much yet. In 1982 Mark Sundberg published the journal "The Analysis of Verbal Behavior." The research within this journal is the basis of what the Verbal Behavior teaching methods are. ABA became popular thanks to Lovaas's article published in 1987 called "Recovery." After this came a book by Catherine Maurice called "Let Me Hear Your Voice." This is a touching story by a mother who had recovered her two children with autism using discrete trials. Many parents wanted what was described in this book and thankfully this helped get the word out on ABA. Unfortunately, this book did not include Verbal Behavior methods such as manding.

All behavioral approaches came into the mainstream professional communities carrying the baggage Skinner had brought with him. The 1970s was the height of his unpopularity. He was still seen as the man of the Skinner Box, who saw humans as no more than big rats. He was the behaviorist who believed only in environment, and denigrated anyone who thought any type of behavior could be determined from within. Skinner's name had become synonymous with extremism. His work was interesting, and one might find a stray idea here and there that was useful, but some felt behaviorism was seen as a discredited theory that would soon fade away.

For these reasons therapists hesitated to identify their methods with his name, and any moves toward applications of a wider range of Skinner's principles were discouraged. Many ABA therapists working today that I've spoken with have only been trained in discrete and mass trialing, and have little awareness of more effective Verbal Behavior methods that have been discovered. Many parents think that these trials are the whole of ABA. Nothing could be further from the truth.

***

In his introductory speech at the New Jersey conference Dr. C touched on all of this history, going into some parts in far more detail than I have here. He showed us that discrete or mass trialing is simply an extended set of procedures based on certain principles of Applied Behavior Analysis, but they are not meant to be an entire teaching approach in an of themselves. They are tools, and as such, they are a portion of ABA. Over the years I have heard many parents describe these trials as if they *are* ABA. This is not so.

Dr. C went on to outline methods and therapies that had emerged from these experiments and programs. He was extending the ideas of Skinner and his successors, using the idea of adaptability to discover what works. He told us we had to take Grier's advice, and teach like strategic scientists: we must learn from our children. I thought of how much I'd been watching Anthony, always searching his responses for clues. I knew that I had been at my best when I was being most observant. I learned the most about how to help my son when I watched my son. What I was hearing here made sense in our lives.

Dr. C started talking about the way all this research had been applied. He explained how many administrators, teachers and therapists weren't aware of the whole of the research. They would hear of a method, hear of its results, and not be exposed to (or sometimes simply not grasp) the context. Many hadn't researched Skinner. Few were aware of the work coming out of Western Michigan U, and some hadn't even heard of Lovaas.

Due to poor interpretation many therapists and "consultants" used simplified portions of ABA, sometimes learning, then performing, gaudy tricks that looked like they were producing genuine results. This was fine for a demonstration, but in the long haul several children didn't generalize. Many therapists were well-meaning, but in the end those that were only performing the discrete and mass trials were doing little more than getting a child to parrot a word that had no meaning.

Lovaas published information on this that popularized ABA. He also developed a program book for therapists. The methods he described used discriminative stimuli (SDs) and trials, but there was nothing about Skinner's analysis of Verbal Behavior. Many therapists that had a lack of education, and only knew the trials, and not what lay behind them resulted in poor ABA programs. They couldn't adapt what they were doing to a given child because they had never been told that was possible. Many of them used the term "SD" without even knowing that it meant. The term "Discrete Trial" became a recipe. You sat the child in a chair, took out your drill book, and so on, through the steps. The rest was supposed to take care of itself.

I heard this, and thought: That's what I'm seeing with Anthony. This is a perfect description of his normal session: they sit him in his high chair, open up the book, and get down to business. If he screams, they might wait until they can hear themselves talk, but then it's just on with business. Their thinking is: this has worked in other cases. The deaf heard something, the mute said something. As long as a child progressed a little—communicated a little—that was better than nothing... right?

This is what happens when an approach becomes systematized. Someone gets results that are a little better than what they'd had up until then. Others hear it, try it, and see the progress. "Here's something," they say. "Here's hope." From there it mushrooms, and the fanfare surrounding it drowns out anything else, sometimes for decades.

A half century before my son would have been given up for lost. Three decades ago there would have been therapy effective enough to allow for some basic communication, but it would have stopped there. And here it was, more than a generation later, and there was the possibility of spontaneous communication, and even conversation, but most people were still caught in the skill set of that earlier era.

A part of this is systemization—where a method becomes a slave to the system it serves, but interpretation also plays a role. Mistakes in interpretation occur when someone notices a new wrinkle or behavior emerging, and asks: "What does Lovaas say about this?" Their teachers can't think of anything in the system that applies, so they say: "He didn't address it directly, but surely he would say..." Then whatever conclusion they reach there on-the-spot is passed on as: "Lovaas said..." In this way the system twists the original thoughts of its founder.

Much the same thing happened to Catherine Maurice. In her book "Let Me Hear Your Voice," she looked at many of the methods known at the time. In many ways her book is dated. She had praise for Lovaas and his ideas, and she had her own take on what parents and children could do to overcome autism. But she too has been the victim of poor interpretation. Maurice's book serves to inspire us, but many take it as a reinforcement of Lovaas's trials, and nothing else. Some criticize the book for this, while others use it as an endorsement of the narrower views of ABA. In the area of autism therapy we should read any work in terms of what was known when it was written.

***

To many ABA became a mantra. Your child has autism? Try Applied Behavior Analysis. The idea was: here was this condition that shut a child away from the world completely, and it had always been considered incurable. Now came a therapy that might open things up just a little. A mute child might finally say a word or two. A seemingly deaf child might raise his head to your voice. Wasn't this incredible progress? And there were those few miracles: children whose eyes opened wide, who eventually spoke in logical sentences, and even the rare case who recovered and went on to college. In a world of dark mystery, this was hope.

But sometimes a small step can stifle a larger one. As we have seen that was the case here. The autistic community reached out for the miracle of a few spoken words, but in their efforts they missed the fact that they were only seeing one part of Applied Behavior Analysis. In doing so they overlooked the most promising tool of all: Verbal Behavior.

As Dr. C put it, they ignored the functions of knowledge in favor of the structures of it. We want to hear the words so much that we lose sight of their meanings. From this comes the mechanistic approach that reminds us of the voices of robots in old science fiction movies: monotone recordings. When you imitate a word just to get a reward unrelated to the word's meaning, that's not as valuable as when you say a word spontaneously because you want the object that the word represents. This is the function of language—why we speak. A lot of discrete trial or mass trial programs concentrate on the structure of language but not the function of it. They don't set up situations where the language matches the action and objects. If a little girl says "candy," just because she's told to, it doesn't mean much of anything, but if she says "candy" because she wants a piece of chocolate then she's communicating something useful. She's telling you what she wants.

This is what we do with typical kids: we teach them language by encouraging them to ask for the things they want. If a child spits out a bite from a hot dog every time we feed it to him, after awhile we'll feed him something else, and the subject of hot dogs won't come up too often. This child's first words are not likely to be "hot dog." But if he can't get enough of pizza, and wants it for every meal, he's probably going to try to say its name pretty quickly. Kids know what they want and don't want, and we use this to teach them language. Without even thinking about it we ask them "wh-"questions. "What do you want to eat?" "Where do you want to go?" "Why do you want to do that?"

According to Dr. C we should never lose sight of the "wh-" questions. What does the word mean? Who or what is being named? Where does the idea or image fit? Why does the word matter?

To bring these questions into real application, the forms (words and phrases) must occur spontaneously. A child must learn to ask for the thing he or she wants. Only in that way is the child going to learn to speak first. When we are young, and we learn to walk, we do it because we want to go places and get things. We learn to talk for similar reasons.

As my friend, behaviorist Alexis Higgins Battaglia told me: If you're going to Italy should you learn the Italian words for colors, shapes, and animals? Or do you want to learn how to ask for a room, hail a cab and order a meal? It's a lot more important to find the restaurant, and get there, and eat some of that great Italian cooking, right? So why would it be any different for children with autism. Once they figure out that there's a way to get what they want, they'll try to do it. We just have to listen, help and encourage them.

***

Dr. C went through all this history, noting how most therapy got caught up in the form and structure in the 1970s and 1980s, then simply froze there.

To all of this we have to add the sudden increase of autistic children in the 1990s. As the decade went on the number of autistic births doubled, then doubled again. Now, by some estimates, there are seven times as many autistic children being born each year. I've already written of why I think this happened, but there are also the results of this explosion.

The first is a huge market for treatments and therapies for autistic children. As the number of autistic children rises, so does the number of therapists. The process begins in the pediatrician's office. She isn't to blame. She diagnoses a condition, then sends the child to the next stage: a specialist, or perhaps a local program. More and more autistic kids are coming in the door at that program. They have to hire more people. The therapists who are already there are inundated, yet they also have to take the time to train new therapists. They use whatever methods they know, and they train the new people in those methods as quickly as they can. This doesn't leave much room for innovation.

In such a hurried process shortcuts are inevitable, and after awhile cutting corners becomes habit. Parents desperately turn anywhere. People without proper training or credentials set up shop. Some interpret what they've learned badly. Others have barely learned anything to begin with. At this point, a mantra like "ABA" becomes even less than a mantra. It's just a slogan on a business card.

***

Dr. C went on to discuss Skinner's original analysis of Verbal Behavior in some detail. Skinner said that every word has several meanings. While a typical child gradually catches on to the various meanings through experience, context and simply by asking, the autistic child's ailment doesn't typically allow for this scope. We come to see a word as having its various meanings by generalizing about it across a spectrum of meanings and their contexts. What does the word do or mean in this situation? What does it do or mean in that one? We may not articulate these questions, but we do search for their answers. When we do this we are looking at the function of the word—what part it plays in our world.

So a word is not defined by its form, it's defined by its function: what it does. Skinner's terms become the language of verbal behavior because of what they do, so a "mand" relates to the action of requesting, and "tact" is in the category of labeling, etc.

Verbal Operants are as follows:

1. **Receptive Language** is following instructions or complying with the request of others. Examples: "Give me the candy." "Show me the candy."
2. **Receptive by Feature, Function and Class.** This is responding to items in the environment when you have been provided a description of them, but not their names. Example: Pointing to the candy when someone says "show me something that is sweet to eat."

3. **Echoic** is repeating precisely what is heard, usually immediately after hearing it. Example: When the child hears "candy" (when that is the discriminative stimulus, or SD), the child replies, "Candy."
4. **Motor Imitation** is copying someone else's motor movements. Example: Giving the sign for "candy" when someone else signs, "candy."
5. **Mand** is asking for things that you want. Example: Saying, "candy" when you want it.
6. **Tact** is naming objects, actions, relations, properties, etc. Example: Saying, "candy" when you see candy.
7. **Intraverbal** is answering "wh-" questions, or having a conversation in which the things you say are determined by what the other person says, even if the subjects under discussion aren't present. Example: Saying, "candy" when someone else has said, "What's your favorite thing to eat."

As I heard all this the light bulbs kept popping on in my head. So much of it made perfect sense in terms of what I'd seen in the last few months. I thought back to the therapists going through trial after trial, and of Anthony's sobs. I thought of all our struggles to communicate with him, and of his own attempts to get through to us.

So much of Anthony's "progress" was merely the notations his therapists committed to paper. He'd mastered this drill or that one. But none of those applied to daily life. What progress he was making in his day-to-day activities was unrelated to what was happening in those trials. Anthony couldn't extend the skills he was getting from his therapists because they had no relation to the things he wanted and needed every day. The therapists said he would start this generalization, but it wasn't happening. The two simply didn't mix. I'd had the feeling this was true, but I hadn't been able to define why. This was my answer. Suddenly I saw that ours was a perfect example of a poor ABA program.

I wasn't about to accept such a situation for Anthony. My therapists were decent people, and competent within the narrow confines of their training, but they had been roped in by a failing system. With an overloaded system people are given only the methods that are tried-and-true: "This helps... a little." They'd been trained to tell people like me: "Just be mom." I didn't mind being mom, but this mom was going to learn all she could possibly learn about how to help her son. I wanted to explore every avenue, and examine every possible therapy. Most of all I would be a strategic scientist, and watch Anthony. My son would be my teacher, and, as his student, I would gather together every bit of valid information I could find. This was a course where I had to get an A.

CHAPTER OBSERVATIONS

The ABLLS (Assessment of Basic Language and Learning Skills) protocol is an excellent tool for measuring your child's skill levels. With it you can determine where they are typical, and where they are behind. This becomes a parent's yardstick for making plans and setting goals. Another good tool is the video "Teaching Verbal Behavior." I suggest parents get both of these. B.F. Skinner's original text, "Verbal Behavior," is very dense reading, but if you want to try it; it's still in print. All three are available at www.difflearn.com.

In 1982 Dr. Mark Sundberg started a journal called *Analysis of Verbal Behavior*. This journal began publishing the papers of various researchers who were working in VB. Many of the methods Dr. C talks about were published there, or in the *Journal of Applied Behavior Analysis.* Dr. Sundberg and Dr. Jim Partington also wrote a book called: "Teaching Language to Children with autism and Other Developmental Disabilities." This book is parent friendly! It helped me understand Verbal Behavior. Many VB teaching methods can be found in their published research, and in the publications of their colleague, Dr. Jack Michael.

***

The following can be useful for both parents and teacher/therapists:

Setting up a good ABA program using Skinner's analysis of Verbal Behavior requires several steps: It is important to get a board certified behavior analyst to set up the program.

First the teacher or therapist should do a *reinforcement assessment* with the parents of the child to determine what the child likes. You can find this at www.poac.net or www.verbalbehaviornetwork.com. Then the teacher/therapist should *pair* with the child. *Pairing* is building a bond with the child. You have to show the child that you are the giver of good things. When the teacher walks into the room the child should see the teacher as a "big chocolate chip cookie." What are the child's favorite things? Bring some of these, and provide them with no expectations or demands. If the child loves balls, bring a bag of them, and give them to the child one at a time. Remember: Each time you hand something to the child that adds to the process of conditioning yourself as a reinforcer. If the child loses interest in the item don't force it on them. Move on to whatever is motivating them at that instant.

Do not underestimate this. Pairing lays the foundation for a good teaching relationship. Though the process of establishing yourself as a conditioned reinforcer (someone the child wants to see, and is willing to learn from) may look trivial to an outside observer, it is essential to making the child into a willing, happy learner. A happy child will progress faster than a screaming child. Pairing yourself with these positive items conditions the child to see you in a positive light. Avoid pairing yourself with things the child dislikes, especially at the beginning.

As a parent you may have seen ABA discrete trial/mass trial therapists do the opposite: walk in, take away toys and other positive distractions, then place demands on the child. That was my experience. The first day of therapy Anthony was up in his chair, TV off, away from anything he liked, and there was the red book of drills. This was how every session started. It wasn't long before the sight of the book and the therapist sent Anthony into a screaming fit. When you think about it, it makes perfect sense. Maybe I should've been screaming too.

Our programmer said that all children cried for the first two weeks. "This is normal" she told me. When we think this way is it any wonder that autistic children avoid us?

The pairing process could take a couple of days or a couple of months depending on the child's history with teachers. If the child is older, and has a long history of teachers who haven't paired with them, it will take awhile. But, as my friend, Regina Cioffi puts it: "This is an investment of time!" If you take time to pair with a child you will get much more from them later. Pairing also brings great natural eye contact. If pairing is done properly there is no need for the "Look at Me" program later. (So in the end it might save time.)

Teachers and therapists should build a rapport with the child. Contrive as many situations as possible to reinforce good feelings with the child. Mom or Dad might help with this by keeping special toys and treats aside, so the therapist or teacher is the only one that gives these items to the child. This ongoing process promotes social skills.

Even after you are paired and placing demands on the child you should always start each session with pairing.

Feel out the child. If they are avoiding you then it's time to re-pair. Pair throughout each session to remind them you are a giver of good things. Continue to offer a variety of preferred items/activities until the child approaches you willingly.

Be prepared to switch the items they like to avoid satiating them on a single thing. I love chocolate but if you kept giving me chocolate over and over eventually I would get sick of it. Don't require the child to request (mand) the reinforcer while pairing. This turns a joy into an effort. Don't approach the child while they are engaged in an activity. Don't chase the child then block the child from retrieving an item just so that you can deliver it first. Never take an item away from the child, then require them to mand for it before returning it. This would make you a taker not a giver. You have started the pairing process when you are a conditioned positive reinforcer to the child. Then the child will approach you willingly. When you do begin to place demands start with easy ones. Prompt the child if necessary. Demands should only be placed while the child is still motivated. The number of demands should be increased gradually.

You can also pair up new toys and activities with reinforcement to try and get the child interested in new things. For example if the child loves M&Ms then offer the M&Ms while introducing a new game. Sing a favorite song the first time you put the child on a swing. Give the child a favorite toy while introducing a new video. This will help to expand their interests.

The same principles apply to peer pairing—the pairing of children with other children. Set up a situation where one child delivers a reinforcer to another child. Make sure you quickly reinforce the child who is the giver as well. For example if Johnny loves trains, have Emily hand Johnny a train, then quickly give Emily a chip for doing this. Then have Johnny hand Emily her favorite toy, and reinforce Johnny for doing this by giving him a stuffed animal. This will help them develop an interest in one another. Once two children are paired shape this into more appropriate play by having them request (mand) from one another for favorite items. Eventually you can shape this into group play activities. This looks funny at first but it is a very effective way to improve social skills. Pairing is powerful.

During pairing assess the child's skills for the ABLLS. Familiarize yourself with the ABLLS so if you see something the child is capable of at the end of the session you can shade it in. The ABLLS should also be worked on after the pairing process. Get feedback from current teachers, therapists and from the parents to help complete the ABLLS assessment.

Manding came next for Anthony. "Mand" is a word that Skinner made up which means command or request. When I first heard about manding I immediately wondered why I hadn't seen it in Anthony's therapy. It was because his therapists had never learned how to use it. This is one of those places where "just being mom (or dad)" should mean trusting your own ability to find out what your child needs. Like Dr. Spock said: "You know more than you think you do."

You need to be a part of your child's teaching. In fact, you can't avoid it. You are already being a behavior analyst whenever you watch your baby's behavior, and figure out what he wants. We watch their body language, listen to their wordless sounds, and try to understand them. Often we succeed. That is analyzing their behavior. Every scream, every sudden, bright-eyed look, every coo, and every tantrum is a possible manding opportunity.

A therapist might say: "Don't worry, he mands all day. We don't have an official manding program or keep data." That's fine if the child is effectively requesting what he or she wants, but what if the child is aggressive and isn't spontaneously requesting? Then concentrate on manding makes perfect sense. All of us mand all day long. I mand for the car keys. You mand for a book. My daughter mands for a TV show, My son mands for a CD. We bring in Skinner's word: *mand* when there's a problem, and some kind of therapy or reinforcement might be needed. If we have to use the word, then it ought to be part of the program.

But manding shouldn't always be a part of some clinical process. It should be done in the natural environment so you can follow the child around and see what he wants. That's where you'll see the difficulties presented in the real world. If you teach pointing when you're offering two items at once, the child may not know how to apply what he's learned in lessons. He may not know that he's being asked to identify a real thing that goes with his real desire. He may not even see that a choice is involved. Anthony didn't. What happens in the real world when "I want" is met with "You choose"? That's when you must refine the process, and help your child identify what he wants.

Anthony could point and identify in therapy sessions. They gave him 100%. But the lesson never left that room. You have to follow them and contrive situations to teach them at the moment when they grab for something. Unfortunately many programs only teach them to respond to our demands.

Look at these exchanges:

The therapist says to a little girl: "Touch the cat."
The girl touches the cat picture.
The therapist says: "Clap your hands."
The child claps her hands.
The therapist says "What color is this circle?"
The child indicates red.
The therapist says "Get the letter A."
The child picks up the letter A.

The therapist always speaks first. This is what the child learns, then we wonder why she isn't spontaneous. We haven't taught her to be. Teach the child to speak first. Teach her to mand. Teach her: I talk, I get.

I studied Anthony all the time trying to understand what was going on in his head. I watched his finger rise into this fake pointing position. He did it because he was told to but he never knew why. To my son this was nothing more than a finger with a nail and a knuckle. The fact that we all point to the light, door, cup, phone and so on, was nuts to him! To Anthony it was just a finger no different than my elbow!

My son did not think in a general way. He wasn't wired to do it. He thought literally. I tried to teach him "who Mommy is." I sat there saying "Ant, where's Mommy? Here I am." Then I'd tap on my chest. In the end if you asked him: "Where's Mommy?" He would look down and point at his chest. I'd just spent an hour teaching my son that his chest was called "Mommy." Our therapist taught him that a picture of a cookie was called "cookie." God Bless the children who can generalize that, but what about the ones who can't?

CHAPTER EIGHT

As I was driving home from the workshop I felt excited. Having had two long days surrounded by people whose focus in life was treating autism had gotten me going. For a whole weekend I'd been able to examine the problem itself. I'd done that in an atmosphere of concrete hopes and genuine accomplishment. These people had seen kids make tremendous progress; they had witnessed the miracle, and stripped away its mystery, making it something that could happen to any autistic kid if only the right methods were used. That kid could be mine; Anthony could recover.

Those were my thoughts driving through New Jersey toward home.

Then I arrived at our house and opened the front door. There were Austin and Daniella running to greet me. This was new to them: Mom coming home after a whole weekend away from them. They couldn't remember the last time that had happened, and now here they were, with all the things they'd saved up to say to me. They both said a thousand different things at the same time. I hugged and kissed them, and tried to listen to everything at the same time. Slowly they wound down.

Then I saw Ant. He was sitting, watching TV. He hadn't even noticed my entrance.

"Anthony?" As I said it I walked toward him. He didn't look up. "Anthony." This time I said it louder. He didn't seem to hear. By this time I was next to the TV. I shut it off. "Hi, Ant." Still my son didn't look at me. I watched him closely. Suddenly my stomach felt empty. I had the feeling that anything I said was being swallowed into a soundless vacuum. Ant's eyes seemed glassy and distant. He was not there.

I looked at Don. "What happened?" I asked.

"The other day he grabbed Daniella's milk cup," he said. "Before anyone realized it he'd drank a lot of it."

"How?" I cried. I wasn't exactly sure what a cup of regular milk would do, or if anything else related to the incident would cause this. All I knew was my son, who'd been beginning to hear his world, and respond to it, now stared blankly into space.

"I didn't see it until it was too late."

"But—how could you?"

"I just missed it. I wasn't looking."

"Not looking?" I suddenly realized that my voice was almost a shriek. Austin stood in the doorway staring at me. His eyes were sad, scared. I thought: "Get a grip on yourself." I saw the communication book that Ant's therapists wrote in. I walked over, and opened it, to see what comments were there.

"Anthony cried a lot during his session today," Stacy had written just hours before. "He had a hard time with any kind of structure. He only wanted to do things by himself, and jumped from one thing to another."

I stood there, realizing my husband hadn't done anything wrong. Mistakes happen. Anthony had drunk regular milk for the first time in months, and now he was having a reaction. That little drink could change him that much.

As I set the book down I realized my palms were clammy. I was nervous. How long would this last?

The only way to answer that question was to wait, watch and do whatever we could to repair the damage. That night Anthony was cranky and aggressive. He wanted to be left alone. Whenever we tried to engage him he would cry and walk away. Just trying to touch him set him off. I tried, heard his cry, then watched as my son turned from me. I wanted to cry.

Later I wrote in my journal:

"June 17, 2003-- I was away a couple of days. When I saw Ant I told Don I was sure he had gotten into something. He had. Now he seems distant, unresponsive, fidgety and irritable. Just not there. On Monday his therapist, Susan, said he was cranky and staring while on the swing. I never saw this, so I brought him outside after she left and he does get mesmerized by the chains of the swing next to him. He is in a trance, staring as the chains cling clang while he swings. You can't get his attention. Not even for a second. He had two sessions today and neither went well. The therapists said he cried and was hard to keep focused. I could tell he wasn't there. Another therapist, Carolyn asked me: 'What happened to Anthony last Friday? He wasn't himself. He wouldn't make eye contact and he wasn't able to concentrate or focus.'"

***

For the next four days I held my breath and prayed. This was new territory. We had done such a good job of controlling his diet, but now I was seeing what could happen with a single mistake. It was as if all the progress we'd made in the previous few months had been reversed.

The days passed. As the week stretched on Anthony gradually recovered. Finally he was alert and focused again. Though I would have preferred to never have tested his diet, this incident showed me it was working. Now I knew that diet had a real effect, no matter what anyone in traditional medicine told me. After this experience I understood more clearly than I ever had that we had to be strict with Anthony on the matter of food. It showed my family too. None of us wanted to lose Anthony again. That single glimpse of his unrecovered persona was enough.

This was the first instance where I got the feeling I was in a tug of war with autism. Here was this force that had pulled him away from me and the world. I had pulled back, and I'd brought him part of the way, but as soon as we let autism have the slightest grip on its end of the rope, it tugged him across the line in its direction. It was as if autism was an entity—a palpable enemy that constantly had to be opposed and outwitted. Yet this sense of opposition defined my mission for me. I was inspired.

Once Anthony was back into the recovery mode I began to feel better myself. Good feelings produced more good feeling—a snowball effect. As long as he'd been withdrawn I'd felt jittery and frayed at the edges. Now some of the enthusiasm I'd gained at the conference came back to me.

The emotional blow of his regression had been doubly sudden and sharp because of its timing. Here I had taken my first trip away from him. I had gone to a place where hope was set out on a counter, wrapped up and put in front of me as if it were a Christmas present. At the conference I had sat, nodding my head, listening, as Dr. C and the others had made point after point, all adding up to me as: "Recovery." And now I had come home to the vacant stare of a child who might as well have gone untreated since birth. It was a heavy dose of reality.

Furthering that sense of burden was Anthony's therapy. For three days I'd heard the whole, long story of how autism had been identified, and how the educational community had dealt with it. I'd heard about the successes and failures. I'd learned something about the reasons for both. The conference had presented me with a vision of what could be and what should be. I now knew that the mass trialing did far less than was claimed to solve Ant's problems.

So many voices at that conference had made so much sense. I'd seen what to teach and when to teach it, and maybe most important of all, how to teach it. I'd learned about the taproot of these methods and therapies: Verbal Behavior. I'd come to recognize how important it was to make the methods positive for the child. You had to let him like what he was doing.

In that weekend I'd come to see Verbal Behavior as the necessary compliment to diet, supplements and other biomedical interventions. Those healed the body. Verbal Behavior could heal Ant's mind, allowing him to communicate and learn just like other kids.

But how could I get that through to the therapists in Morris County, New Jersey? How could I break the bureaucratic inertia that forced potentially good therapists to use ineffective methods? How could I change the daily grind that Ant was going through, and replace it with methods that worked?

I felt like someone fighting a battle in a jungle. I was stuck in Morris County where ABA was nothing but trialing, with therapists giving signals, then training children to parrot proper responses. I'd heard that south of us, in Brick Township, they used the Verbal Behavior methods I'd heard about that at the conference. But my battle was here. I felt as if I were slogging through swamplands and jungle. Any jungle fighter will tell you: the battle is for hearts and minds, and you can only win over one village at a time. So it was for me and Verbal Behavior: the methods would only take hold as parents fought the battles one county at a time. My job was here, in my county, with my son.

That was what I saw as my son slowly returned to me from that one glass of milk.

Once I saw that Anthony's diet was back on course, I couldn't wait to tell Anthony's therapists what I'd learned about Verbal Behavior. I began talking to Stacy and Susan about everything I'd heard at the workshop. They were both curious, and even supportive. Unfortunately, neither of them knew about Verbal Behavior.

I could see I had a task ahead of me. I would need to do thorough research, and help these two figure out how we could bring Verbal Behavior into Anthony's world. I called the Verbal Behavior Network.

"You need to get Anthony's therapists trained in a Verbal Behavior approach," said the woman on the other end of the line.

"That's what I figured," I said, "but how?"

"Let me see," she said, and I could tell she was looking up something on her computer. "I'm afraid there aren't many Verbal Behavior-trained people in your part of New Jersey. Maybe if you call your early intervention provider they will know someone. They should."

I thanked her, and did as she said. "Why would you need that?" asked an administrator.

Behaviorists and teachers were discussing it for an entire long weekend. The progress they described was incredible."

"I'm sure it was," she said, "but I'm sure they have their problems too. We don't recommend anything like that until a child reaches school age. At that time it might make sense. You've only had your son doing ABA for a few months. He's not even two yet."

"He's old enough," I asserted, though I wasn't sure how I could back that up. Up to then no one had told me that a child had to be school age for Verbal Behavior, and in my mind it didn't make sense. Wasn't it a given with almost all of these general programs that the earlier we got to the child the better the results? I was pretty sure that was true, but I couldn't say why or how with any real certainty. Instead I tried a different argument. "ABA is a lot of things," I said. "The therapy he gets now is only one very limited part of it. Verbal Behavior methods are ABA too."

"Yes, well, the trials are an ABA method that we've found to be tried and true with children his age," she said. "After all, we've had our share of successes too."

"My son isn't one of them," I said.

"You simply have to give it more time."

"But he hates it."

"I know," she said softly. "Ms. Burnett, I realize you want to do everything possible for your son, but you have to give our therapists time to produce results. We can't always perform miracles, but I think, if you have patience, you'll surely see results. In the meantime it's important that you be supportive. That's what moms can do: be moms, with all the love and care that brings with it."

"Yes, I know," I said, "but this is a case where your therapists would like to learn this method and try it on Anthony."

"I can't just change what they're doing," she said. "I'll tell you what: I'll have a coordinator from our agency come by and talk with you. You can tell her all your concerns and she can evaluate the situation, and maybe recommend something."

I agreed to this.

The coordinator was no more help than the voice on the phone. She was trying, but she couldn't quite see what I was talking about. We sat talking as Anthony played with some toys. "Exactly what is it that you want to change about his program?" she asked, her eyes shifting from him to me.

I sat there under her gaze, trying to put my feelings into words. "I don't want him to scream and cry. I don't see how sitting him in his high chair, then waiting till he's quiet, then getting him to touch his head so he'll get a cookie does much good. For all I know he might think his head is the cookie, or that one always goes with the other."

"But from what I see in his reports he's making progress."

"He is," I said. "He's brighter, more active, and he listens better. But he's not really learning to communicate anything that means anything. Everything he has learned stays in that therapy room. He doesn't generalize it" As we talked Anthony rocked himself back and forth, and smiled. He looked happy and healthy, which didn't exactly help things.

"But being bright, more active," she said, "those are great improvements. Some autistic children never do that much."

"I know, and I'm very grateful that he's improved, but I think that's because of changes we made in his diet."

"How can you be sure of that?" she asked.

"I've seen it. My whole family's seen it, and so have his therapists. Look at their reports from mid-June. It's right there. He'd been making steady progress for weeks, but then suddenly he was unresponsive. It took him a few days to pull out of it. We hadn't let him have dairy products in months. As soon as we'd taken him off of them he'd started getting more active, more alert. That was before the therapy even started. Then one day he gets hold of a glass of cow's milk, drinks it, and ka-boom! The change was almost immediate. He just sat staring ahead, hearing nothing, just like before."

"Yes, well, I'm sure a good diet is important, but that may not be the whole of it. You say you don't want him to cry, and you don't want him to point at things for rewards, but what do you want him to do? Exactly what kind of therapy should we be giving Anthony?"

"I'm not saying those things are bad in themselves," I said. "I'm just saying that if you have a case where they're not working, it may be time to try something new, and recently I saw something that was new to me. It's what I heard about at a conference down in Monmouth: Verbal Behavior. It's based on the work of a man named B.F. Skinner. He wrote a book about it."

"But the therapy Anthony's getting is related to that. Exactly what aspect of Verbal Behavior are you talking about?"

"I'm not sure," I said, "but I know that what he's getting now is missing some of the things I heard about."

"Well, we're always willing to listen," she said, "but if we're going to make changes we really need something more to go on. I wonder if you might not do better just to wait a little while longer, and see what develops from what our therapists are doing now."

"The therapists are interested in learning more about Verbal Behavior," I said.

"So am I," she said. "And when you have a specific program for us we'll be glad to look into it for you."

"I'll—I'll find one," I said, though I wasn't sure how to do this.

That was how we left it.

For me it was back to my research. I read more books, and devoured information on the Internet. I came across an organization called LEAP (Living Equally Among Peers) that had recently begun in our area. It had been founded by therapist, Alexis Higgins Battaglia, who was also a behaviorist. Alexis had been working with another group called POAC (Parents of Autistic Children) which had been started by parents such as Tom Caffrey. LEAP was an offshoot of POAC and Verbal Behavior Network. Tom had an autistic daughter, and he too was a behaviorist.

Through both of these groups Alexis and Tom were working to bring Verbal Behavior programs into our part of New Jersey. They were planning a series of free workshops to our area where parents and teachers could get training in the methods of Verbal Behavior; however the first workshop was still six months away.

Lacking any other way to get immediate action, I reviewed everything I had learned, and told my team I wanted to try some manding with Anthony.

"We can do it through sign language," I said. "It's something I heard about at the conference, and I've been reading about the ways to do it. That way we can get past this business of simply pointing at something for a cookie."

"He's gotten good at that," said one of his therapists. "So maybe he can do more."

"I'm sure he can," I said. "What we want to work toward is getting him to use sign language directly for the thing he wants right at that moment. That way the sign has a definite, here-and-now meaning, and our reactions will be more like real communication."

They agreed that that approach made sense. With a new program, and their skills as therapists, we started working on the signs for music, swing, cookie, water and chip. The first sign Anthony picked up was "swing." In no time I was saying "swing" and then signing it, and as soon as Anthony heard and saw the sign he would run to the back door to go out to the swing.

His trialing continued in the therapy sessions, but they worked on manding too. I kept manding with him throughout the day. Pretty soon it seemed like a natural way to train him to express his wants and needs. He didn't learn everything right away, but he was picking up things.

It wasn't all easy. Anthony developed some sensory issues. He began to hand flap, and he wanted to hold a spoon in each hand all day. Without the spoons he stumbled dizzily sometimes, but when he was holding them he regained his normal coordination. I wondered if his equilibrium was off. He didn't feel secure in his own body. He also became fixated on his peg board. He would play with it all day if I let him. He also began to grind on sand in the sand box. I would try to redirect him but at every chance he had he would grab a handful and put it in his mouth to grind on it. The therapists wanted him re-evaluated by the occupational therapist. She came to our home and assessed him, and said he could use some occupational therapy. I agreed. She began coming twice a week to work with Anthony. I'm not sure the therapy helped much, but she taught me some important points about Anthony's sensory problems. She said that his resistance to being cuddled was more defensive than anything else. It was all about keeping the world at bay. If his mind couldn't process what his senses were telling him, then all that information was threatening. That made it important to develop behavior that would keep the sensory overload to a minimum.

It was one more piece of useful data. In those early months, having no access to formalized Verbal Behavior therapy, I took whatever knowledge I could find, wherever I could find it. It was like assembling a puzzle; if I could just find all the pieces I might be able to come up with a coherent strategy for defeating the enemy—autism.

Despite our lack of formal programs we were making progress. On July 13, 2003 I wrote in my journal: "Ant has been signing really well. He now knows "music," "swing," "water," "jump" and "cookie." He still needs some prompting. He has been alert but also hand flapping with his hands when he gets excited. I keep trying to think of what we might be doing different to cause this. Ant has been so cuddly lately. He rests his head on my shoulder and I can even sit with him like this. He stays put. He never did this before unless he was sick. I'm enjoying it. Today he even hugged me and patted my back. It was so cute. He has been jargoning a lot and it seems he is trying to talk. He tries to sing the 'Dora The Explorer' song by saying: "Ba pa, ba pa." His sense of humor is developing as well. He is a little comedian. He tries to make us laugh. He will tease us, and be silly while watching to see if we are laughing. He definitely seems to understand language more in the past couple of weeks. I think the signing is helping this."

CHAPTER OBSERVATIONS

The therapists in Anthony's program were working on pointing. Pointing is the most rudimentary kind of sign language, but it doesn't promote speaking like sign language can. Sign language can help children express wants and needs, just as pointing does, but it can also deal with things that are more abstract. Once a child begins to learn signing there is the potential for expressing almost anything. For non-vocal children sign language is the key to day-to-day communication.

But how well does sign language fit with children who are vocal, and have the potential to speak. Do they come to rely on it, thus discouraging speaking? I don't think they do. When we only teach children pointing as a method to request something that limits their communication. With pointing the object must be present, or within a proximity that they can clearly point in its direction (perhaps in a closet, or the next room, or outside). Pointing is frustrating, and sometimes completely useless if you can't find the object the child desires. You may wind up rooting through closets and drawers with an increasingly agitated child on your hands.

Pointing is fine at the start. Most of us do it automatically, and for a child with autism it is a perfectly good beginning. This didn't work for Anthony. We worked on pointing constantly, he didn't understand. As the child wants to express more, you will need to augment his or her communication with larger and more expandable tools. Language is expandable, or *augmentative*, because it involves large numbers of words or symbols which include actions, objects, intents, desires, and timeframes within their meanings. Also, they can be assembled in different ways to express different things. Pointing can't do all of this. Sign language and speech can.

So where should you go with the child? Sign language or picture selection? When choosing an augmentative system, look for the one that is easiest for the child to learn. A system that requires the least effort is often the best. Does the child have the tools necessary for this system? With sign language a child needs hands. Can the child use this system to respond? In sign language response is the single step of forming the appropriate sign.

Compare that to the picture-selection system, which is based on pointing. If my son wanted juice he had to get his book (which wasn't always handy) open it up, flip through the pictures, find a picture of juice, take it out, then find an adult, hand it to them, and the adult would get the juice. Look at all those steps—eight of them. That's more than some people need to do their taxes. This isn't a communication device given to discussing complex emotions, and it's not all that easy for getting a cup of juice either. If my son can sign, and wants juice, he finds me, signs "juice," and I get it for him. It's simply more efficient.

Also, signing allows for verbal behavior across all the meanings of words (mands, tacts and intraverbals). It's closer to actual speech. Speaking is topography based as is sign language. You can have a conversation and express your feelings using sign language. Pointing or picture selection is not topography based. When my son points at a picture, he's showing me an image that someone drew of the juice he wants. I recognize the image, and respond accordingly. But when he signs, he is forming the symbol himself, just as we pronounce words as symbols for the things they mean. Not only is he forming this symbol himself, but in signs he has symbols for things that can't easily be pictured. He will soon simply be able to say he's thirsty, and he wants to drink something. If he wants grape juice instead of orange juice he won't have to find a new picture. Soon he can sign about the whole subject in terms of the action of his drinking, rather than simply the drink itself. In all of these ways the system has allowed him to augment what he was telling me, and that is much more like speech.

Talking and signing are almost identical forms of verbal behavior, while picture selection is quite a different form of communication.

Signing is not difficult to learn. Many children with autism, including many with motor imitation difficulties, can learn to sign. You don't have to be fluent in sign language to use it with your child. You just have to stay one sign ahead of them. As you see a possible future target for your child than you can look it up. If you go to www.verbalbehaviornetwork.com they have a free site with several signs.

Sign language training may fail for a number of reasons. Do not start with signs like please, yes, no, help, toilet, more, thank you, give me. These are too complex. You have to understand quite a bit of language both receptively and expressively to be able to understand such complex language. The first signs taught should be specific mands only.

Other difficulties can stem from not providing the child with enough opportunities for manding, or from not putting the signing into practice outside of therapy. As soon as a child starts learning signs in a therapeutic setting, you should start encouraging the child to sign in daily activities. When Anthony was learning to sign for water, I would practice with him during meals by pouring him a sip of water when he was thirsty and having him sign. At the end of the meal he did it at least ten times. Also, during his bath he loved to watch the water fill up the tub. I would shut the water off, he would look at me. This was another opportunity to practice the sign. He would sign water and I would turn it back on for ten seconds. I would shut if off again and repeat.

Another problem can arise when you continue to rely on prompts. If every communication starts with a prompt then you make the child prompt-dependent. This is when a child gets stuck at one level for too long, with no progress toward the next one. This is also why many children are not spontaneous. We don't set them up to be spontaneous. If we always talk first as teachers, or grab their hands to prompt them a sign first...the children learn to wait for us to speak. We are actually teaching them not to be spontaneous. For example, "What do you want." We want to show them to act on their inner craving for something. You may be focusing on labeling, but not manding, or you may not be generalizing the signing process to other people in your child's life. If you are going to use signs then the people who have the most contact with the child (it could be parents, grandma, siblings, therapists, teachers) should all learn the child's signs. This is how the child learns to generalize the verbal behavior, communicating with a variety of people instead of just one. This also applies to setting and times. If you only sign at meals, the child won't necessarily generalize the behavior enough to use it during playtime, or when you're walking down a street.

Before you teach a non-vocal child sign language sanitize the environment. Put the items you're going to use (child's favorite items) in clear containers, in sight, but out of reach from the child. If the child has everything he wants right there with him, he won't need to communicate anything. This way it gives you opportunities to teach your child to ask for items. The child must convey his wants to you if he's going to get anything, however make it easy and fun for the child.

Manding should be taught in the natural environment. Begin teaching with the item present. It helps if it's an item that can be broken down into in pieces, such as chips, or blocks. This gives you several opportunities. The teacher holds all the items. Sign and say the item as you take the child through each of these next steps. Make sure the child is motivated to have the item by delivering one piece freely. If they take it you'll see that they want it. At that point model the sign with your hands, while saying the word. Next make the child's hands form the sign, helping to shape their hands into the sign if necessary, again while saying the word. Finally quickly give the item to the child, also while saying the word.

Go through these steps quickly, saying the name of the item with each step. I practiced with my husband first. You go quickly so you reinforce the child ASAP, without frustrating the child. By saying the sign as you are signing you are pairing up the vocal word with the sign. This will help the child learn the word, in the hopes that he or she will eventually say it. As you do this again and again you should reduce your prompts. Reduce the physical guidance first. (This act of reducing is called "fading," which is reducing an action gradually, or in baby steps.) Try to fade your full physical prompt to a partial physical prompt as quickly as possible. To do this make sure you touch the child's hands as lightly and as little as possible. The partial physical prompt may become nothing more than lightly tapping the child's hands together. If this does not work don't hesitate to use more of a prompt and try to fade again later.

Eventually fade the partial prompt. Wait a few seconds after you model it and before you touch them to see if they can do it on their own. Next you will need to fade the model of the sign. You model and the child imitates. Bring up the item, then wait a few seconds. If the child does the sign for the item, give it immediately. You may want to say "What do you want" to the child as a prompt. However, fade out, saying: "What do you want?" before the child mands to teach the child to initiate and be spontaneous. To fade this out; try holding up the item without saying anything. If that doesn't work you can fade out slowly by decreasing the statement each time the child mands. For example say: "What do you..." then "What do..." until you don't have to prompt them at all. Finally you will fade the item being present at all, and wait for the child to ask for it on their own, but don't expect children to be able to mand without the item present unless you have already taught them to.

Always fade gradually. Do this with both prompts, and with the proximity of the item. You might keep the item in your closed fist while asking them what they want. If they don't seem to, flash the item and ask again. Then put it behind your back, in a bag, or in a cabinet, giving them more and longer chances to mand. As you make the item more remote, fade the prompts. Don't overcorrect them. If the child is approximating the sign accept that, and reinforce it. It is the idea you are trying to get through to the child that communicating is valuable, easy, and rewarding! You can shape the sign up properly later.

Your point in all this is to reinforce the child's attempt to communicate. You should keep data on manding. One way is with the kind of counter clicker that you can get at office supply stores such as Staples. They also sell them at www.difflearn.com.

In the beginning you will want to click every time they mand. The goal is to increase the mands per minute with each session. Later, when they are manding more regularly, without much prompting, you will want two clickers, one for the mands you've prompted, and the other for the mands they make on their own (independent). After awhile a child will usually mand as much as 500-1000 times per day. Think of how much your family mands in a day. For me it's "Mom, can I have a drink", "Mom, where's my hat", "Mom, can you help me?" Imagine a day without requesting anything from anyone! Typically you mand all day! This process will teach them the function of the word instead of just the structure of it. The functions of words have been ignored. Imitating a word just to imitate, is not as valuable as saying a word spontaneously because you have a motivation for it. This is the function of language. Why we speak! A lot of discrete trial or mass trial programs just concentrate on the structure of language but not the function of it. They don't set up a situation to make language "useful" for the child. The child can become robotic and imitate language but it is not used by the child spontaneously. For example just saying "candy" because a teacher said to say it rather than the child craving a piece of candy and being able to say "candy" because they want a piece of candy.

CHAPTER NINE

I liked the holistic pediatrician Anthony and I had seen in April, but she was more of a general holistic pediatrician than she was a specialist. I had been reading more about the various groups that concentrate on autism, and I had discovered Defeat Autism Now, or DAN. This was a group of medical professionals, scientists, and parents who had banded together to share information, and promote the most effective use of the new programs and therapies dealing with autism. The more I read, the more I liked their approach. Without being reckless they examined cutting edge ideas in the field of autism, then put those ideas into practice. Theirs was an aggressive approach.

As I considered what had happened with Anthony, balancing the areas where he'd improved against those where there hadn't been much progress, I knew that's what I wanted: medical professionals who were training themselves specifically for the fight against autism. I wanted people who weren't afraid of new ideas, and who were already practicing methods which had proved to be effective. I needed people who were as proactive in their medical approach as I was in my approach as a mom. I was beginning to realize that Anthony only progressed when I stumbled through barriers, rather than just standing there waiting them to fall.

I wanted Anthony to be examined by someone familiar with the DAN protocols. I made an appointment with Maureen McDonnell. Maureen is a registered nurse and also acts as director of her company, Health Education Services in Pennington, New Jersey. She coordinates DAN conferences nationwide.

Working with a cofounder of DAN, Dr. Sydney Baker, Maureen counsels parents about biomedical approaches to treating children with autism. Dr. Baker has written extensively about autism. That's what I wanted: the people who were writing the things I was reading.

It wasn't easy. I had a lot of paperwork to fill out. As I went down the forms, filling in answers, I realized I had never been asked such specific questions. These people wanted particulars about all sorts of details. What did Anthony eat? What did he seem to hear? What was his reaction to loud noises? What did he tend to focus on in particular situations? This was the first place I'd gone where they asked for Mom's "observations and opinions" right on the form. "Hey," I thought, "these people think 'just being mom' might include being a close, accurate observer. I like that."

I also liked the fact that they were interested in details of his diet. It has always made sense to me that a doctor would begin with a patient by asking what they eat each day. After all, the things we put through our bodies are likely to have a huge effect, right? Habits, exercise, and reactions are important too. To a large extent we are what we eat, and we are what we do. This seemed to be the thinking behind the hundred-or-more questions on the form.

I got an appointment in September at the end of the summer. Don was off traveling, so when the day came my cousin, Sharon, came with us. I felt I needed an extra set of ears.

"I'm nervous," I told Sharon.

"Sure you are. Anybody's nervous going to see a new doctor or therapist. Don't worry."

"I know, I know..."

We went through the door into Maureen's office.

She was one of those medical professionals who understood nervousness. The place was set up to ease the mind, and make a mother feel comfortable. The scent of burning candles put me at ease, as did the decorative borders of herbs on her walls.

"Sit down, please," she said.

Sharon and I sat, but Anthony didn't. The new environment had him going top speed. He fixated on the Venetian blinds, and started climbing the chair to get at them. We got him down from there, but he wasn't finished. He looked around for anything he could get into. Sharon did her best to keep him contained so Maureen and I could talk.

Maureen watched Anthony, but didn't seem at all bothered by his behavior. She seemed to want to hear anything and everything I had to say, and to observe everything she could about him. She seemed to do all of this automatically. Her serenity was impressive.

She looked at the paperwork, and we went over Anthony's diet. She looked at the range of supplements he was taking, and gently quizzed me about his health history. I told her everything I could remember.

The first thing she focused on was the onset of autism in Anthony. "He's one of those who didn't show it at birth," she said.

"No," I agreed. "Not at all."

"And he had all the vaccines?"

"Pretty much as soon as our pediatricians felt he should have them," I said.

She shook her head. "The things they tell us to do. It seems wise at the time... And then he started showing symptoms at seven months."

"I wrote it down for you," I said, pointing at the forms. "There were ear infections, a cough."

We went over all of it. Her questions were to the point, and she was a good listener. She was especially interested in Anthony's reaction to dietary changes. "He perked right up, did he?"

"Yes, as soon as we got him off dairy. And once, when he got hold of some milk, it set him back four days. That was early this summer."

She nodded. "It's amazing what a few simple dietary changes can do, both for good and for ill. It sounds like you're using that to Anthony's advantage."

"We're trying. It's the one thing that seems to really work wonders."

Finding a medical professional that paid attention to obvious cause-and-effect was like opening a window in a stuffy room. This was such a nice change from conventional doctors. Maureen gave me some lab kits to take home. These were tests that would tell her more about exactly what was going on inside Anthony's body, giving her a baseline for further treatment. There were blood tests along with urine and stool.

"We'll look at the results in light of this history," she said. "Once we know exactly where he is, we'll know better how to get him where he ought to go."

"Where should he be going?" I asked.

"Well, we hope that he'll move toward being a healthy, normal little boy. I certainly think that's possible. You've already done a lot of things right."

As we drove home, Sharon said: "She seemed awfully nice."

"Really," I said. "And the way she listened. That's one of the big differences between the traditional people and the ones who are really shaking things up. The traditionalists tell you to listen to them. The experimenters want to hear everything you have to say."

"It's too bad it has to be so experimental," Sharon said.

I shrugged. "If they're right about what causes it, this is a new kind of autism. Most of the cases in the last decade or more are this new kind. But it's got them trying new things, and that's good for every autistic kid."

"I hope it works," she said.

"So do I," I replied. My mind was on all the testing we would have to do once we got home.

In the following days we did a stool test to see what kinds of bacteria and yeast were in his stool and to what degree. It also showed us what the bad bacteria and yeast was resistant to, and what would kill it off. For example would the antifungal medication, nystatin, work on killing off the yeast? Or was the yeast in Anthony's system resistant to it? That would mean he needed a stronger medication.

It's best to develop a strong and slightly raunchy sense of humor while working with these lab kits. The stool tests had Don and me dissecting the contents of Anthony's diaper. At first it grossed us out, but once we inured ourselves to the task we had to laugh, voicing questions a mind couldn't help but ask. "Where did this come from?"

We did a urine test to analyze for peptides, those undigested proteins from casein (dairy) and gluten (wheat) foods. Those peptides are what I've already described as having drug-like effects on autistic children. You can collect the urine either from a bag you place on the child or let your child go without the diaper and follow them around with a cup waiting for them to urinate. In either case we realized it went easier with a sense of humor.

We went to a local hospital for the blood work. The first blood tests were to measure Anthony's mineral levels. We also did blood work to get an IgG response food allergy profile. This was a profile drawn up for testing for intolerances to certain foods. IgG allergies are those that result from long-term intolerances. Unlike the IgE allergies that make us immediately break out in hives, or swell up our lips, or make our eyes itch, IgGs are the ones that have more subtle, long term effects. The symptoms might be headaches, brain fog, or irregular bowels, or gas, just to name a few. Often we don't relate these to food, but they are intolerances as surely as a shellfish allergy that swells up your face in a minute. The hospital staffers were patient and helpful. Though Anthony fought, he still let them manage to do their jobs. It was hard for me, as it always is for any mom. I just kept reminding myself that he needed this work. I thought about how routine these feelings were getting. I'm not sure if that made it any easier though.

We had other tests to take home in kits, and we did them over subsequent days and weeks. It was five weeks later, well into the fall, that we had our second appointment with Maureen.

All the results were back. The blood tests showed that Anthony had an elevated level of peptides, bad bacteria, and yeast overgrowth. He also had an IgG allergy reaction to bananas, cashews, cheese, coconut, corn, egg, peanut, canola, sesame, soybean, walnut, wheat, and Brewer's yeast. Maureen suggested that I eliminate these foods for several weeks, and rotate all the other foods in his diet. I was to make sure he got all his nutrients, but I wasn't supposed to feed him any one food too many days in a row.

In the course of the food rotations I was supposed to add back the foods that Anthony hadn't been able to tolerate, but I was to do so slowly, reintroducing one food at a time. With each addition I would carefully gauge his reactions. Maureen and I agreed that Anthony should only eat those foods where he had no visible reaction. As long as no reaction showed up he could eat that food, but I had to make sure he didn't overdo it. We would check his IgG once a year, and see where we stood.

Like everything else about autism treatments, it was a juggling act. One thing a parent should be ready to learn is how to balance things. This is most obvious in food, but it's also true in therapies, supplements, and everything else. You will always be checking to see your child's reaction, so you can know if you are going too fast or too slowly, or if you're giving them too much or too little. Once again, this is where we all have to be strategic scientists. We must pay attention to the child, and learn from every reaction.

I realized that Maureen was a strategic scientist, but she hardly seemed like one. Through all of this she was warm and very helpful; she recommended that I make an appointment with Dr. Neubrander.

So finally it was time to see a doctor who I'd read about. Dr. Neubrander is one of the best known DAN doctors. I called his office and made an appointment for Anthony. Dr. Neubrander was in demand, so it was going to take awhile. They gave us an appointment in December, almost two months away. However, in the meantime his office didn't ignore us. They sent literature, and several pages of questions. The questions had me going into minute detail about everything I'd done with Anthony up to that point. I told them about dairy products, GFCF, vaccinations, therapies, and everything else they wanted to know. I soon felt as if I were writing a long novel. Of course, it didn't have an ending.

At this point I was glad I'd already gone through so much in the process of filling out forms for Maureen. That had been a little like training camp for the forms with Neubrander. Though the paperwork was overwhelming, I was again impressed with how much specific information he wanted. I had a feeling he would use this information, and possibly see patterns that I hadn't yet detected. I felt I was on the right track.

There was also plenty of literature accompanying the forms. It was a mix of hard information, and comforting testimonials from parents. I didn't worry about the promotional stuff. I had read some of his work, and talked to professionals and parents alike about him.

In 2003 Dr.Neubrander was known for his research into Methylcobalomin B-12 (Methyl B12) injections for autistic children. Methylcobalomin is a form of vitamin B12 that the brain needs. It is essential to keeping our biochemical paths functioning properly. Otherwise the body suffers. A lack of methylcobalomin B12 can be a cause, or further irritant in autism, Alzheimer's, ADHD, cancer, cardiovascular ailments, and other diseases.

Our appointment came at a moment when Anthony was in the midst of a bump in the road to recovery. At such moments the bumps seem like boulders. A parent can only hope. In October 2003, nearly two months prior to our appointment with Dr. Neubrander, Anthony's constipation had returned. Again he would have to strain while trying to have a bowel movement. Once again we were faced with having to give him enemas. His stool would then come out sometimes hard like clay and other times soft, with mucus and foul odors. I couldn't figure out why. I hadn't changed anything in his diet. I was sticking to the gluten-free casein-free (GFCF) diet religiously. I had also removed corn and soy months before, having learned that some autistic children had problems with both. I wondered if it could be starches such as rice or potatoes. This new mystery bothered me. It seemed like no matter how much we progressed, something new came along to make him suffer. Seeing this made me physically ill.

Anthony's therapist had told me of a mom she knew, Laura, who was also very interested in the biomedical approach. She said Laura was going the gluten-free casein-free route, as well as using several vitamins and supplements. She felt that Laura could use some support from someone who was dealing with similar hardships, and asked if she could give her my number. "Of course," I said.

My therapists had given my number out to others moms before but the moms rarely called. Even when they did, they were not usually interested in biomedical approaches. Often their pediatricians had cautioned them against dietary changes and supplements—the same warnings I'd heard. I was the one who would bring it up, and that part of the conversation would end, more often than not, in frustration on my part. Though I could point to my own son as evidence, these moms trusted doctors more than other parents. That is the strength of the medical establishment's authority, something doctors should consider when making blanket pronouncements.

Only a few hours after I'd talked to the therapists my phone rang. She introduced herself, and said: "I have a son with autism named Rocco. I'm pregnant now—our second, and if you want to know the truth I'm scared to death. I want to know more about all this."

"When was your son diagnosed?" I asked her.

"A few months ago. He was eighteen months. He'd been fine on his first birthday, hitting all the milestones they talk about. I was watching, and it seemed like things were good."

"Was he talking and pointing?"

"Oh, yes," Laura said. "He was doing all those things—making sounds, some that sounded like words. He could show you things he wanted. He seemed like a normal kid, doing all those normal things."

"And now he's diagnosed with autism," I said, knowing all the horror and sadness that lived in those words. "Believe me; I know what you're going through. So what do you think happened?"

"The day after his first birthday I took Rocco in for his one-year checkup. He got two vaccines that day: MMR and chicken pox. I didn't worry about it. I figured it was all for the better. Boy was I wrong."

Laura explained that after that Rocco developed chronic diarrhea. "That worried me, but what was worse was the way he responded to things. He started slipping away. Every day he faded a little further. Within a month he was gone—no eye contact, no response when we'd say his name, no pointing—it was like a whole part of him just vanished out of this world, and what was left was just a shell."

"Oh, my," I said. "I know this so well. With Anthony it started at seven months."

"Do you think it was vaccinations?" she asked.

"I think they had something to do with it," I said. "Them and antibiotics."

"I've been reading," she said, "and I'm sure it was them."

As we talked I realized I hadn't met another mom whose story was so similar to my own. Laura had incredible drive in her ambition to get her son back. She was willing to do anything. I knew that feeling perfectly.

Laura also had an appointment with Dr.Neubrander set up for December. She lived only a few minutes from me. All these parallels led us into a close friendship.

I can't overemphasize the importance of knowing, and talking to others who are going through this. Comparing notes helps, both in terms of information, and in keeping up your spirits. This contact helps you fight the lonely, sad feelings that you'll get on a bad day, and it amplifies the elation when things go well. Who else is going to be properly impressed when your little boy waves bye-bye for the first time? Who, other than another parent, is going to realize how much work, therapy, and hope went into that single moment? Who else is going to understand that you have a two-year-old who is working as hard or harder than any adult with a fulltime job, simply to achieve the simplest communications skills?

An autistic child seems to put a parent on another planet. Just as the child's world has narrowed, so has ours. But with other parents with autistic children our perspective spreads back out again. The experiences of others will teach you, and often give you hope. You'll be glad to lend an ear, and whatever knowledge you have. In return they will do the same for you. At such a point you realize that the friendships forged in crisis are often the closest ones. In that sense I've treasured my friendship with Laura, and with other parents as well.

I've mentioned the little things like a bye-bye wave, but there are so many other parts of life where the difficulties become second nature, and the tiny steps of progress must be celebrated as if each one were leading to a pot of gold. I think of the dread I could feel approaching family gatherings. I grew up in a loving family, and I've always looked forward to seeing everyone, both on my side and on Don's, but what happens to such feelings when you know each meeting will bring the pain of seeing your nieces and nephews soar right pass your child? This isn't something anyone has to mention. It's there in every child who runs and takes cover in a game of hide-n-seek, and every shout of "You're it!" in a game of tag.

I watched these kinds of moments again and again, thinking of Anthony's therapists, and the endless trials, ten times to each one, in an attempt to form the most basic skills. I watched, knowing there was this idea of Verbal Behavior that might change Anthony's whole world, but I couldn't find anyone who could take us there yet. At such moments you hold your breath, and search your soul for patience. Other parents might lend a sympathetic ear, and give me heartfelt words of consolation, but Laura understood.

We think of a child's second birthday as a moment of celebration, but Anthony's depressed me. I saw an imaginary clock above his head, ticking away. I kept thinking: "Time is running out. If we can't get him on track soon a lot of the damage will be permanent." I pictured what my little boy should have looked like on this day. The previous months had been so full of research, and battling both the disease and the lowered expectations of so many medical traditionalists, that I hadn't really sat and looked at exactly where he was, and where I had wanted him to be. I hadn't reflected on what I was doing, against my ideas of what I wanted to be doing. And I hadn't allowed myself to even begin imagining an older Anthony, possibly not recovered, with autism still clinging to his appearance, and his every movement.

Suddenly I found myself thinking: "What if my son doesn't come back? What if he never speaks? I'll forever wonder how his voice would sound. What does he dream of? What does he think about? I don't even know what he wants for his birthday." I looked at Anthony, my birthday boy, and tears welled up in my eyes. "This," I thought," might be our son—forever!"

My sister-n-law, Renee, called to wish him a happy birthday and I couldn't help myself, I cried. Don's mom called and I cried. I couldn't control myself. I was not usually this way. On most days I was full of hope, and my conversations would be peppered with "when Anthony gets better." I was so busy figuring out ways to help him, and sharing those ideas with friends and family, that I didn't give myself time for any pessimism. I never acted downbeat.

But there, with my son turning two, my eyes ran like a faucet. I was crying all day. I couldn't turn off the sadness. I found myself wondering how long these feelings would last. There they'd been, ruling my thoughts for just a few hours, but they felt like they might be there forever. I felt tired and depressed but I also kept telling myself that I had no time for this.

Anthony had been holding his spoons all day. That didn't help. This was one of those symptoms that I'd seen more of lately—this and toe walking. Toe walking was when he would walk on his tiptoes, as if the soles of his feet were uncomfortable. It made it seem as if walking flatfooted made him feel insecure, or even in pain. The spoons appeared to be a part of a balancing act, as if he might fall over without them. He gripped them in each hand. I could tell that Anthony didn't feel grounded in his own body.

His occupational therapist had told me that it was common for autistic children to lack an awareness of their body in space. That was the reason for the spoons—they were a little like anchors. Still I hated them. To me they were like a symbol of all that was wrong. He would hold one in each hand for hours. He would not put them down unless I took them away. When I finally did take them away he would keep his hands in the fist position as if he was still holding them.

I didn't know what to do about the spoons, or about my own feelings. As Anthony lumbered around, led by his spoons, I felt embarrassed. Somehow they kept him from looking anything like a normal two-year-old. It was like a ten-year-old sucking his thumb, or a grown person dressed in a diaper. There was nothing funny in it.

At one point I called Laura, and described all of this to her.

"I know," she said. "I feel it with Rocco, and I'm sure it'll be hard when his birthday comes. Will it ever end? How could you not have those feelings? Two years—it's supposed to be a landmark. I guess most moms complain about the terrible two beginning."

"I wish I could complain about that," I said.

"How true," said Laura. "I wish I could too. Are you having people over?"

"Everybody."

"Are you cooking?"

"Sure. I can't get away without cooking. Hey, I'm Italian, you know?"

"Okay, what are you having?"

"Eggplant parm, sausage n' peppers, pasta..."

"Sounds like a great meal for depression. You must have a cake."

"A big one."

"Eat an extra slice for me."

Talking to Laura helped a little. Some months later she told me that talking to me that day had helped her prepare herself for Rocco's second birthday. Birthdays are always hard. You want the one to come where you're looking at a child who's just like all the others—and you want it now.

But I cooked and ate, and had some cake, and it was over as fast as it had hit me. Suddenly it was the next day and the depression was just a lingering memory. I had a lot to do. I showered, then started into the huge pile of paperwork I still had to finish for Dr. Neubrander. It was my full time job just as much as it was Anthony's, so I just kept moving.

After a couple of weeks Anthony's bowel movements still hadn't improved. It was the beginning of December, and our appointment with Dr. Neubrander was still weeks away. At that point Anthony started vomiting, and his face was almost yellowish. I took him to our regular pediatrician.

We might have gone to the holistic pediatrician, Dr. M, but so much stood in the way of that. This was one more of many instances where I had to think of insurance factors. Medical insurance is weighted almost completely toward traditional medicine. Some alternatives have made their way into some policies, but holistic treatments weren't covered by ours. Also, his regular pediatricians had a large practice, with 24-hour service. Dr. M was one person, and could only keep normal business hours.

The pediatricians said Anthony probably had a stomach flu. I went along with that diagnosis, but wondered if there weren't more to it. He hadn't had a bowel movement in days. That night we gave him an enema and he passed a clay ball. He perked up for a couple a days but with no bowel movement. He looked almost mushy, and he was pale. We went back to the pediatricians and this time they suggested that it was an ear infection. I totally disagreed with this. Anthony hadn't had an ear infection in eight months and I knew his symptoms for ear infection very well. He would pull on his ear, get a high fever, and cry with pain when he tried to sleep. He was not doing any of this. He was lifeless, and he'd begun vomiting again.

Don and I drove him to the emergency room. There they did X-rays, ultrasounds and a cat scan of his abdominal area. The ER doctor determined Anthony had a severely impacted, yet loose stool.

"His ears are clear," said the doctor, "but one ear has scar tissue."

"He had a lot of ear infections," I said. "From seven weeks on he had them, but not so much lately."

"The scar tissue must be from that," said the doctor. "That's probably why your pediatrician thought it was infected. The scars can make it look that way. Anyway we'll see what we can do about his stool."

Three enemas and twelve hours later they still couldn't get him to go. They had one last thing to try, but if it didn't work they would have to operate. They inserted a tube in his rectum, and pumped in saline. We walked him around and prayed. A nurse who'd been with us all day stayed even after her shift had ended. "I want to see it work," she said. "I've been here this long, and I might as well see what comes out."

Finally, he had a huge, muddy stool. The relief was huge, but beneath it lay that thought of what would happen tomorrow, the next day and the day after that. Would this just keep happening?

"No," said the doctor when I asked him. He scribbled on his prescription pad. "We'll put him on an eight-week course of Miralax."

I took my son home, better, but now we were saddled with another drug. Miralax, a strong laxative, improved his bowel movements, giving his stool a muddy, sandy consistency. I kept wondering how he would be once the eight weeks was over. I didn't want him dependent on a laxative or anything else.

Soon it would be time for his appointment with Dr. Neubrander. Laura and Rocco were going there for their first appointment a week before us, but the day before they were scheduled, Laura went into labor and delivered her daughter, Francesca. Her husband, Rob, took her place.

Laura had been nervous about having another baby. She was afraid that this would happen again. I couldn't blame her. Don and I had always thought of having four children until autism struck; now we thought differently. If I were to have another child I'd be terrified that autism would strike again. There are many cases of more than one autistic child in a family.

The day after Laura delivered Francesca by caesarian my phone rang. "Christie it's Laura, are you busy?"

"Where are you?" I asked.

"I'm at the hospital. I've been reading all the stuff from Dr.Neubrander."

"You just had a baby, and you're already working on reading all of that?"

"What else do I have to do? Rob took Rocco to his appointment, and now there's all this stuff to read." Laura filled me in on the details of Rocco's appointment. Rob had brought her a pile of new literature. Trying to make sense of it overwhelmed her, but still she wanted me to get an idea of what to expect at my appointment the following week. Her preview helped.

The next week, when Don, Anthony and I arrived at Dr.Neubrander's office he was with another patient. Anthony played with the water cooler in the waiting room. It was a Saturday morning, and there wasn't any staff in the office. The other patient left and Dr. Neubrander called us back.

He was a no-nonsense scientific type, giving an air of absolute competence, but not that much effusive warmth. It wasn't that he didn't care. I felt as if he cared a great deal, but professionalism was a large part of who and what he was. It was a change from the appointments with Maureen. In some ways he was intimidating. But he seemed as determined to help these kids as anyone could be. He had analogies for everything. He would give you the medical terminology for a treatment, but follow it with an analogy that made sense of what he'd just said. This helped me understand. He focused on Methycobalomin B-12, explaining that we should give Anthony a trial period of injections. He didn't want us to make any other biomedical changes yet. We would record everything, both positive and negative, from the injections. He went into detail about the methylation process and how Methy-B12 worked to make autistic children's brains function better. When he talked of its potential I could see he was truly excited.

He had more lab work he wanted to do, and he laid out exactly what we would be doing in future appointments. The appointments would come every five weeks. There would be phone consultations as well. He covered diet, supplements—everything. He couldn't seem to impress us enough about the exact method of filling out paperwork for his appointments. He liked things in a certain order. Though I respected the fact that he took this so seriously, I was a little amazed by all work. His regimen was so strict that he reminded Don and me of the "Soup Nazi" on Seinfeld.

"If we don't keep good records I think he's going to fire us," Don said.

It was okay with me. I felt like Lincoln must have felt when he finally found Grant—a general who was willing to try to win the war, and not just fight holding actions. At last we had a doctor who really wanted to fight autism with every resource he could find. If the price was paperwork, I would do paperwork.

CHAPTER OBSERVATIONS

Methyl- B12 is the key to biomedical interventions in autistic children. Without it the biomedical approach won't do much of anything. To understand this it's best to think of the brain as a road system. These roads are the pathways for brain signals, and for the chemicals and nutrients that keep the brain going. They not only carry our conscious thought processes, but they also carry the everyday substances and signals that keep our bodies and minds working. So if you think of the brain as a big interstate system, some cars and trucks are hauling ideas, memories, and plans, while others are transporting the signals for your next breath, your next heartbeat, or your next bead of sweat. These chemicals, nutrients and signals are all a part of a biochemical mix that creates and carries energy and information.

Among the most important ingredients in this system are amino acids. These are the building blocks of the proteins necessary for life. Certain amino acids are manufactured by the body. As long as we function we keep making these, but sometimes we don't make enough of one or another of them. We need to be making enough of each one. There are other amino acids that we don't make in our bodies. To get these we have to eat foods that contain them. For most of us, if our diets are right, we get enough of these. They combine with the amino acids that our bodies make, and everything works fine.

There are amino acids that we get from food that are necessary to proper brain functions. These include methionine, which acts as a kind of gatekeeper and fuel depot on these roads through the brain, and glutathione, which is more like a street sweeper. The methionine is there at certain junctures, acting with the other amino acids to make sure they've got gas, as well as an up-to-date road map. The glutathione pushes obstacles out of the way.

In autistic children these processes have been interrupted. For one thing the balance of metals in the system has been disrupted. When there's a buildup of these they create road hazards on the pathways. The glutathione gets rid of excess metals, including mercury. Once again, the methionine helps the glutathione get where it's going so it can do this essential clean-up work.

Methyl B12 makes sure there's plenty methionine in the system, and it creates the conditions for the body to make enough glutathione, and for that amino acid to be able to do it's work. The methylation process is necessary in the proper function of both of these amino acids, and when a child has autism, methyl B12 injections are usually the only guarantee that methylation will take place.

In a brain affected by autism these two amino acids need a boost. The body has to be stimulated to produce enough glutathione, and needs an ample supply of methionine from the outside. Methyl B12 injections serve both of these purposes. With the injections the brain gets the right mix of ingredients to clear the roadways, fuel the cars, and make sense of the roadmap. That way other essential substances and signals can start moving to the right places again.

Methyl B12injections provide sulfur components such as thiol. Thiol helps detoxify the body, but it also has an adhesive quality which helps hold proteins in the proper shapes. The injections also stabilize homocysteine levels. One of homocysteine's functions is to act as a back-up to methionine.

Giving an autistic child vitamin B12 orally doesn't do the job. Autistic children usually have problems with digestion, some of which I've already mentioned. These problems often block the absorption and conversion of the vitamin into methylcobalomin through methylation.

When we inject methyl B2 directly, their brains get it directly, and there's no chance for the process to fail in the digestive tract. Dr.Neubrander has found that 94% of his patients respond favorably to this treatment. (DAN 2005 conference manual, p. 223 and "Autism Effective Biomedical Treatments" by Jon Panghorn and Dr.Sidney Baker. Page 59)

According to Dr.Neubrander most children who get these injections become more aware of their surroundings, start speaking, and act more like other typical children. Don't make the mistake of thinking your child won't respond to methylcobalomin injections just because his or her levels of B12 are in the normal range. The B12 may be in the body, but it may not be in its most effective state when it reaches the brain. To see your child benefit from these injections you have to try them. (Material on methyl B12 taken from "Autism: Effective Biomedical Treatments," by Jon Panghorn and Sidney Baker pgs 12-15)

CHAPTER TEN

Dr. Neubrander had given us plenty to think about, and plenty to do. I could see that having him as our doctor would be an education. When he'd gone over his list of what we would be covering in the future appointments it sounded like the most comprehensive approach I'd heard yet. I felt as if I was going over a syllabus with an incredibly demanding professor. That wasn't a bad thing; I felt confident that this professor knew his stuff. But he wasn't kidding around.

His concerns ran from diet to vitamins to supplements, and he knew these would affect every other area of Anthony's life. He talked about amino acids, chelation, glutathione supplements, antifungal treatments and much more. He needed more lab work on Anthony—more data. He wanted to know how things were from one day to the next. He was asking me to observe, and report. It was something like the therapy at home: he wanted me to be a mom, but to him being a mom meant being part of his scientific team. He wanted me to be serious about my job, and if I was, he would take what I said seriously. He didn't just want that; he demanded it.

Our next appointment would be in five weeks, and by then we would all know more about where to go next. This was his normal speed with new patients, but it seemed pretty fast to me, and I liked that. He seemed to have a good idea of where we ought to be going, and though he might be a little like the Soup Nazi in his approach, he was doing it so that he could learn about what was there, rather than only seeing expectations. One problem with many therapists and health care practitioners is that they tend to only see the things that they expect to see. That's not being a strategic scientist.

On Christmas Eve the methyl B12 injections arrived in the mail. Both of us were nervous about giving Anthony the first shot. For one thing, we'd heard that the first shot could produce several different reactions. In the first hours it might act like a stimulant. On Christmas Eve night we didn't relish the thought of Anthony feeling the stinging prick from a needle, then going into overdrive while we tried to put things together for Christmas morning. Also, I don't think either of us was in a hurry to give Anthony an injection, no matter what it was. Anyone who has any squeamishness about shots—giving them or getting them—should understand that. It's an idea you have to get used to, and we wanted circumstances a little more conducive than we had on one of our busiest nights of the year. Anthony's nights were far from perfect right then, but at least he slept through some of the night, and at least we knew what to expect.

So we let it pass, got the presents wrapped, had a good Christmas day, and waited until eight in the evening. It was a stunning night, so perfect for Christmas. We'd had a few inches of snow that day, and a little was still falling.

Outside the world had that kind of sweet stillness the world gets in the evening glow after a snow.

Finally there we were, inside our warm house, with a little boy ready for bed, and a tiny needle full of the mystery of methyl B2. Dr. Neubrander had recommended giving Anthony the shot after he was asleep. He'd prescribed a cream to put on Anthony's skin, numbing the area where we would give the injection. I wondered if the cream was more for our peace of mind than for Anthony. After all, the needle was small. But, small or not, a shot is a shot.

Anthony had begun to wind down from the excitement of Christmas Day, and I was hoping against hope that the shot would be like a nightcap, and put him right to bed. He would most likely wake up during the night anyway, just as he had every night lately, so wouldn't it be nice if he could have some real rest first? And the night, the snow, and the stillness were so peaceful—I couldn't help but hope that peace would hold.

I applied the cream to his skin, then I realized I couldn't do it. Don took the needle, and gave it to him. Anthony squinted. A moment went by, and it was past. The needle really hadn't been much, and I'd been far more worried about it than my son was. Anthony yawned. I think he may have yawned a couple more times in the next few minutes, but those were the last signs of weariness for awhile. He started looking around for new things to do.

Within an hour Anthony was totally wired. He went this way, stumbled that way, pulled at the tree, and generally wreaked havoc. I thought he would climb up the walls. It was well before midnight that Don and I began to ask ourselves: "What did we get ourselves into?"

As we watched this performance we decided to give the shots to him in the morning from now on. Eventually he got to sleep, and so did we. It was well past midnight, but at least he slept through till morning. The next day we wondered if he was a little more leveled out.

"Maybe he's just tired from last night," I said.

"No. I think the shot might be doing this," Don replied.

"I hope so. Anyway, don't you think we should give it to him in the morning from now on?"

Don nodded. "Definitely."

We gave him the shot every third morning.

We quickly found ourselves wanting to keep up with the regimen simply because the changes were obvious. I don't know if the calm we saw the morning after Christmas was directly related to the shot, but other effects couldn't be denied. Later in that first day Anthony noticed our dog, Pretty, at the door. He opened it for him, let him out, then in. Anthony had never done this before. Twice that day he also petted both of our dogs. Anthony had never even acknowledged the pets before. There were other effects that made all of our lives easier. The most immediate of these was in how he slept. Anthony had been back to waking up every night, and we could usually rely on having to deal with a wide awake boy for two hours before getting him back to sleep. With the injections he slept through till morning.

Getting a goods night's sleep made all of us feel better, which helped us notice all the beautiful little differences in our youngest son. Within a few days Anthony began to be more stable on his feet. He climbed the stairs better. He even began jumping in the air. At first I didn't tell his therapists about the injections. I wanted to see if they confirmed my observations. Before long they had all noted improvements. One wrote in Anthony's communication book that she was "amazed at how verbal he is." She noted that he was more focused. Another therapist wrote that Anthony was trying to say words, and was managing to mimic approximations.

The changes kept coming. Anthony needed less prompting when I would mand with him. All of a sudden he was figuring out things that had always been mysteries to him. He didn't always have to do a new task over and over; he would pick it up right away. He did new things spontaneously, seeming to finally comprehend how cause-and-effect works. He began to make connections between actions and results.

In the car driving home I turned on the light, then shut if off. Anthony giggled. I said: "Light."

"Li..." he said, coming close with the word.

I turned it back on, making a funny noise, then flicked it off again.

"Li..." he repeated.

I turned it on.

He knew what was going on.

It was in these types of games that we could see Anthony coming to a new way of understanding. Before it had been slow, and even with that it was hit-or-miss. Now, once he made a move, he immediately grasped that something was coming. Once I saw that, and responded in some consistent way, he could make the connections almost instantly.

He liked this. He seemed to like almost everything better.

"He's so much happier," Sharon commented to me.

"He is," I admitted. "Isn't it great?"

"The other day he kissed me. He's never done that. He's always pushed me away."

"I know. He pushed a lot of people away. Sometimes it seemed like a reflex. But he's a happier boy now."

"That must make life easier," Sharon said.

"You bet it does," I said. "You know, three separate times I've seen him walk up to Austin and give him a kiss. Just a couple of weeks ago there were times when I wasn't sure he was even aware that he had a brother."

"He's getting to be an affectionate little guy," Sharon said.

"I think we're seeing the real Anthony," I told her. "I think he was meant to grow up to be an affectionate little boy. He's more aware of his surroundings, and that makes him more himself-as the world sees him. He's not caught in some little tunnel."

As Sharon and I talked I realized I was describing the son I'd been hoping for from the start—the one I'd thought I'd seen coming those first few months. It wasn't that I'd ever expected Anthony to be some little doll doing exactly what I thought he should do. I had simply expected a normal little boy who would give his mom the normal surprises. I'd figured on mischief, mayhem, laughter, curiosity, and all those things that we think of when we picture a kid being a kid.

That night I watched as he sat in his high chair, studying dinner. He wasn't just looking at his own food. He raised his head, and stared out across the table, regarding each of our plates. His eyes went from plate to plate, and food to food. You could almost see the questions forming in his mind. Was he getting the same thing we were? Did each of us have the same meal as the others? As he ate some of his own food he watched us. What was that thing Austin was using? A fork? What were those round things covered in red? Did they call them "meat balls?" It tasted pretty good.

The next day I caught him examining me as I applied chapstick. Suddenly he grabbed my face, pulling me so he could study me more closely. He touched my lips. He'd never looked at me quite like this before. You know how it is when your child wants to see something up close, and that something is you. Every child does it at some point. But any parent of an autistic child knows what it is to miss that; to sit with your child, having him right there with you, as you study something about your face in the mirror, then realizing that your child hasn't even glanced your way. At such a moment the bottom drops out of your stomach, and you feel that your child is falling into a well, and all you can do is reach down, with no hope of catching him.

And now, suddenly Anthony was right there with me. I was looking at my face, and so was he. Then I was gazing into his eyes, and he was looking right back at me. All the clarity was there, and in that moment I realized how badly I'd missed it. His eyes were truly with me, engaged, and wanting to know. We were connected! I felt as if I had caught him, and now I was pulling him back into our world.

As I've said, it wasn't just me. Don noticed that Anthony was grabbing at his diaper when it was wet.

"I can't believe it," Don said. "Before he'd walk around in the same dirty diaper all day if you let him."

One day when Anthony was sitting in his high chair in our kitchen he pointed across the room. It took me a second for me to realize he was showing us the cabinet where the snacks were. Before this when Anthony had pointed at things it had been in the manner of an autistic child: only things near at hand, so close he could practically touch them. But the cabinet was a good dozen feet away. That distance seemed like a good metaphor for his expanding world.

Not all the changes were so wonderful. As Anthony reconnected not everything was going to go his way, and I shouldn't have been surprised that he had more tantrums than before. In seeing a larger world, Anthony had a better grasp of exactly what he wanted. In understanding cause-and-effect he was probably getting a better notion of what was physically possible. If there were snacks in that cabinet, that meant there was the possibility of having them now. So why wasn't he getting them now?

This was one of those instances of a positive effect bringing some negative results with it. Being more aware, he was not as easily sidetracked. It was a thin, dark lining on a silver cloud.

One day, just after New Year's, Don and Austin started play-wrestling. As they tumbled around on the floor Anthony ran over and jumped on them. They stopped, but he jumped on them again, trying to push them together. He grabbed their hands, pulling them. Anthony wanted to wrestle too! I grabbed the video camera, and started recording it. This was such a perfect example of what we were seeing every day. The tape from that day is still on the

Internet at www.drneubrander.com. If you click on "video," then "recovering children," then "ten months in the life of Anthony" you can watch it yourself. There you will see a picture of a kid who is right there in the moment. While you watch it, keep in mind that not long before this had been a kid gripped in autism's silent stare. You are seeing one of his earliest forays into the world of a normal child, and I think you'll agree: he likes it.

This started happening more often after that. Anthony would start playing with Austin, Daniella, Don or me. Before, whenever there was play, we'd had a hard time keeping his attention. We'd always had to work at it, and sometimes it just didn't happen. Now it was different. Anthony started seeking us out. He wanted to play, and when he played he'd want to keep at it for a long time.

This progress wasn't at all like the fits-n'-starts advances he'd made in the past. For a couple of months it was amazingly steady. We knew that had a lot to do with the injections of methyl B12 simply because it dated from that first shot on Christmas night. That was our family's best Christmas present that year. Those injections were pulling Anthony out from his tiny interior world, and into the life of our family. They made Anthony "available to learn." I often use this phrase to describe what biomedical interventions did for my son.

No longer did I have to practically stand on my head to get his attention. Keeping him engaged was much easier. It made teaching him more fun and rewarding. "Available to learn"-it meant that he was more with us, and with it. He wanted to learn, and he wanted to react to people, and have them react to him.

What it really meant was a whole lot more work for all of us. After all, Anthony didn't suddenly comprehend every little detail that he'd missed over almost two years. There was so much catching up to do. He was like a brand new hard drive: empty and waiting for software. It was time for a whole lot of data entry; it was time to teach. Now I could see the absolute necessity for the learning tools I'd heard and read about so often in the previous year-all under the heading of "Verbal Behavior."

I knew that if we could get the VB going, Anthony would soak up knowledge and skills like a sponge!

CHAPTER OBSERVATIONS

This chapter leads us to the actual practice of Verbal Behavior therapy. VB can be valuable for autistic children under any circumstances, but its effects can be seen most clearly in children who are "available to learn." Methyl B12 is one of those things that can get them there.

All the biomedical interventions I have described are essential to getting the most out of Verbal Behavior methods. Because of this the reader should see this last chapter as being closely linked with the next chapter. Any parent can bring about biomedical interventions with the help of sympathetic medical professionals. However, to start VB methods in a town or county requires the interest of a community of parents and therapists.

I have already mentioned Alexis Higgins Battaglia, therapist, and founder of LEAP (Living Equally Among Peers). Operating in northern New Jersey, LEAP is a non-profit organization focused on bringing free comprehensive training to professionals, paraprofessionals and parents in the autism community. This training stresses Verbal Behavior methods, and their applications in Applied Behavior Analysis. POAC (Parents of Autistic Children) and Verbal Behavior Network were also involved with bringing these workshops to our area. You can find more information about these organizations at www.poac.net and www.verbalbehaviornetwork.com.

CHAPTER ELEVEN

A set of workshops for Verbal Behavior was going to start in our area that February. Northern New Jersey was finally going to get some information about these methods. To me this was a milestone. I'd been hearing and reading about VB for a year. Since the previous summer I'd been in touch with Alexis Higgins Battagila. Though we'd never met, we had emailed back and forth. She had recommended websites and reading for me so I could educate myself about general approaches, and details about VB. She had become one of my main mentors.

At the time Alexis's efforts were centered in areas to the south of us. New Jersey and California were the two places in the country where Verbal Behavior methods were truly making inroads, but so far Alexis and her allies were one small stronghold in one part of our state. I was making it my goal to help her bring VB to the counties in northern New Jersey. For that I would need workshops so I could show people what I'd been hearing about-and so I could learn more myself. I knew how sketchy my knowledge was, and I wanted to learn more. I'd been waiting through the fall and winter, and now I would finally have the chance to get a close-up view of VB along with other parents and therapists in our autism community.

I'd done all I could to let people know, printing out dozens of copies of workshop schedule. I'd handed these to anyone who might possibly be interested, saying: "You really have to see this stuff. We've all got to learn about VB. It makes sense and it really works."

I had faith in it because of the few small things I'd been able to do with Anthony in signing and manding. Those partial steps, and the biomedical measures, were the only obvious causes in his progress. Yet I knew that the things I'd done in Verbal Behavior were only baby steps, taken without any real context. There was a broad program out there, with a whole set of ideas underlying it. I needed to convey that way of thinking to all the people around me: both parents and professionals.

So I was disappointed on that first February evening when I got to the auditorium, and saw no sign of Anthony's therapists. In that moment I felt as if I'd been stood up for a date. I knew they were sympathetic to the idea, but now I felt as if they just weren't quite interested enough to be there. It made me mad.

The turnout was far from huge. As people came in it built toward a group that numbered about 30. Though Anthony's therapists were absent, I was glad to see a number of parents I'd contacted. I missed my friend Laura, but then she finally arrived late. I'd known she wouldn't let me down. I had told Laura everything I knew about VB. I was sure it could help her son, Rocco. But she had never seen any presentations about it, so she was simply one of the curious.

As I sat down I saw a familiar face right there in the row ahead of me. It was my old high school classmate, Marissa, who I'd seen at Dr.Carbone's workshop. I tapped her shoulder. "Marissa," I said, "we keep bumping into each other."

"Don't we?" she said. "Do you know Alexis?"

I nodded. "I do through email, though I've never met her. We've been in touch since last summer. She told me about this. How do you know her?"

"Oh, she's pretty high profile down where I am," said Marissa. "She coordinated the program I'm in. I teach a class of autistic children."

"So you teach using VB?" I asked.

"Oh, yes. That's what it's based on."

"Wow." I said. "That's what we need up here. I'll tell you, Marissa, ever since that conference where we heard Dr. Carbone, I've been reading about Verbal Behavior. I've tried some stuff with Anthony-just piecemeal things, but he usually does respond. I can tell it would work really well if I had a whole, coordinated program."

"That is what you need," she said. "It can't really have its full effect unless you use a total approach. It has to be there every day coordinated into all of his therapy and learning. But maybe it's going to start happening up here. If you can get something like what we've got, you would have the approach you're talking about. It's a really good program."

"All our agencies offer is the old ABA stuff," I said. "I think Anthony's therapists are interested. I was hoping they would be here tonight. They sounded interested, but none of them showed."

"It's not always easy with therapists," she said. "Were all of them really excited about it?"

"I don't know if 'excited' is the word... and their programmer, Jill, hasn't had much good to say about it."

"That can be the problem," she said. "The closer to the top you get, the more traditional the thinking. So many of the administrators were in school a long time ago when ABA was the great new hope. Back then VB was Skinner, and Skinner was supposed to be the guy who raised kids in a box. It's not true, but that's how they see it. They know ABA works better than what was going on a few decades ago, and so they don't see any reason to change."

"But the therapists are younger," I said. "They shouldn't be as locked in."

"I know, but they still have to work for the people at the top. Your programmer is a rank above them. She's probably a part of that old ABA thinking. The therapists may disagree with her, and with the people who head up the agency, but the agency pays them. You've got an exciting idea, but this is their free time, and they're not getting any encouragement from the top, and you aren't handing them a paycheck."

I nodded. "I guess that's true. I'm going to have to be more persuasive."

Marissa smiled. "You're pretty good at that, Chris. Just work on them. They'll be here next time."

"I'll do that," I vowed. This is so important, and I know they are interested. It's just like you say-I didn't consider all that stuff that's working against this. But his therapists have been receptive whenever I bring it up to them. I've told them what I've been learning, and we've started some manding with Anthony, but it's not consistent. We're still doing trials too. No one knows enough to do otherwise. I just wish I had a teacher like you to help."

Marissa laughed, and shook her head. "I've got a lot going on. I'm planning a wedding right now, and at work we've got a waiting list of parents, but you know, I might be able to do something."

Inside I wanted to jump at the offer, but I could tell she was already stretching herself thin. "Uh... let me figure out some stuff first. I won't bug you about it right now-not until we figure out what we need, and what we can get right now. I guess that's part of why I'm here: to find that out."

"Okay, but call me if I can help," she said.

It made me think of how sweet Marissa was, and how so many people in the autism community were that way: always trying to find new ways to help others.

Marissa and I sat back and listened as the program began.

It was my first actual look at Alexis Higgins Battaglia. She stood down on the floor in front of the stage, with a screen behind her. Like every speaker these days, she had a PowerPoint presentation. Hers was well-organized and effective, but the main show was Alexis herself. The woman I saw was short, blonde, confident, and moved this way and that.

It was a night of introduction to the whole approach. I listened to everything she had to say, and got a great overview of the field. She brought it alive in a way that books and websites could not. She looked everyone in the eye, engaging both individuals, and the room as a whole. She had that talent.

I felt oddly shy. Though I can be as assertive as the next person, sometimes I can be overtaken by an odd shyness. Maybe it's a matter of being faced with someone who is making a case for something I want far better than I feel I ever could. She had command her of facts, and a firm hold on her audience. Suddenly I was content to just be a follower.

I hung back, talking only with people I knew. Laura had arrived late, but now she was here, wanting to explain why. I met another mom, Regina. She had a little boy, Thomas, who was Anthony's age. Regina was one of those naturally funny people, the kind who makes you wonder why she's not in stand-up comedy. She had a line for every person, and every situation. "They talk about school," she said. "I haven't even had time to think about it... except that I'm counting the days... and hours... and seconds. My house is a pig sty, isn't yours? With a kid that age who has time to clean? Who even notices? Not my husband. What man notices a pig sty? Isn't that what they lived in before we married them?"

Regina had us all laughing, but she was totally serious about why she was there. Like me, she was ready to learn about Verbal Behavior. Her son was also in a mass trialing Early Intervention program. She hadn't done any biomedical therapy yet, but she was eager to learn. We talked about that, and I told her what we'd been doing with Anthony. She listened and asked questions. "I'm going to try that," she said, "and once I start paying attention again, I'll put Thomas on it too."

She was kidding and serious at the same time. Regina had some medical problems of her own, and the diet appealed to her. In the weeks ahead she did put her son on it, but she also tried it herself, and both mother and son benefited in different ways. Regina didn't need any dietary aids to help her pay attention. She was sharp. That night was the start of a beautiful (if somewhat hysterical) friendship.

Laura had managed to bring Michelle, her EI programmer, along. With the problems I was having with my own programmer's reluctance, I had to admire the fact that Michelle was there. I sat near them, and we all chatted until the video presentations began. Some of the videos were of older children who had never said a word, and might never talk. Laura had a hard time watching this. Rocco wasn't showing any verbal skills yet, and it was hard for her to watch these older children who had never reached a verbal stage. To a parent of an autistic child this is the nightmare: a child who never speaks a word. I felt as if we were sitting there watching a sad movie, the kind that tugs at the heartstrings. Laura cried, and I tried to comfort her.

As the workshop broke up a long line developed. Just about everyone there wanted to talk to Alexis. I still had a touch of the shyness I'd felt when she'd first started speaking. Besides that, I was tired. It had been a long day, followed by all the feelings, and connections there at the workshop. I decided not to introduce myself. Instead I said my good-byes to my friends, and drove home.

***

The next workshop was scheduled for two weeks later, the end of February, but just that one evening, even without Anthony's therapists there, had relit the fire I'd had for Verbal Behavior. More than ever I knew this was what Anthony needed.

I've noted that our EI programmer (we're calling her "Jill") hadn't seemed enthusiastic. Now I spoke to her about it directly. I was acting as a full advocate now. I knew that would bring out her truest feelings, rather than bureaucratic tact.

"It's not really an accepted method," she said. "What we're doing has shown positive results time after time. Can you say that for Verbal Behavior?"

"The people who use it can," I said. "I'm not a therapist, so I don't have the expertise to use it."

"I know," she said. "You're not trained in these things, but if you want my expert viewpoint, I don't think we should use it. I don't see the evidence of what you claim."

"If you would come to the workshops you would see," I said.

"I've spent my life educating myself on these issues," she said. "It's my job. I don't believe in wasting my time. I think you are wasting yours."

This wasn't what I was looking for. Right after that I removed Jill from Anthony's case.

He still had his therapists though: Stacy, Susan and Carolyn. Though they hadn't been there for the first workshop, they could see that I was more enthused than ever. I guess it was catching, because they seemed to be getting more interested.

I gave Laura a call. Though she'd cried at the workshop, it had also impressed her. She was getting sold on VB.

"You met my programmer, didn't you?" she said.

"Michelle? Yes. You introduced us, and I talked to her."

"Well, she's getting into it. She wants to learn everything she can. Why not get her to be Anthony's programmer?"

Why not, indeed? I couldn't believe my luck. Just as

I was losing the programmer I didn't want, the one I needed was right there, ready and waiting.

Before the next workshop I got an email from Alexis. "I noticed your name on the signup sheet," she wrote, "but I'm sure I didn't meet you. I was looking for you." I promised her I'd introduce myself the next time.

When I walked into the second workshop I already had one of the biggest supporters in my life right there with me. My dad had come. He was really interested, and wanted to take notes so he would know exactly what was going on with his grandson. It made me feel good having him there.

This time one of Anthony's therapists was there too: Susan. As soon as I saw her face I smiled. I knew she was there with the support of the other therapists, even if Jill was against it. Now I could sense that Anthony's world was beginning to connect to the things I was learning.

"I feel like I'm undercover," Susan said.

"Why? Because Jill doesn't approve?"

"Oh, yeah," Susan nodded. "You know, a lot of people at the office are down on this stuff, but I'm not. I've been reading, and talking to some people. I think you may be onto something, Chris."

"Let's hope so. Right after I talked to Jill I felt like I'd reached a turning point. Something snapped in me."

"I heard you asked them to take her off as programmer."

"Of course I did, but I don't think they understood why. I'll tell you, it's an honor to have you, and Stacy, and Carolyn. You're all open and ready to figure this out, just like I am. But the agency doesn't seem that way at all. When I talk to them I feel the same way as when I'm talking to the mainstream, traditional medical people-the ones who keep saying diet doesn't have anything to do with it."

"Yeah, you've told me about them," said Susan. "But we've seen what that diet does for him, and the methyl B12 shots."

"I know you see it," I said, "and I'm really happy you do. And I know it's the things you see that make you want to do this. But those people in the offices, and people like Jill, they're set in their ways, and they won't change. They're so pessimistic."

"I know," she said.

"After I talked to Jill I called the office. The woman I talked to called VB the 'flavor of the week.' Right then it occurred to me: What does she care? When she's 70, and relaxing on her pension, a whole lot of moms of kids like Ant are going to still be taking care of their adult autistic children, making their beds, feeding them meals... and she's going to be sitting in a beach chair gabbing with her friends. When five o'clock hits, people like her go home to healthy kids. When the weekend comes they deal with Girl Scouts and Little League. I'm not saying that shouldn't be. I just feel like during their 40 hours a week on the job they should be open-minded to anything that might help. She never gave me a single specific reason why they wouldn't try VB. She doesn't know enough about it to get specific."

"Well, we're the ones there with you at the house, and we'll try it," said Susan. "That's why I'm here."

I thanked her again.

A lot of things came together that night. Michelle was there, and I took the opportunity to ask her if she would act as programmer for Anthony. "Laura told me you're learning the Verbal Behavior techniques, and hey, you're here," I said.

"I am," she agreed. "From what I'm seeing Verbal Behavior is a much better approach than anything I've done before. I want to use it with Laura's son, and his therapists, and I'll be glad to do the same with Anthony's therapists, but I can't do this alone. I'm just learning too. I'm not sure how to coordinate a program in it yet."

"I think I can help there," I said. "There's a friend of mine, a woman I know from high school. I ran into her almost a year ago at a conference, and she was at the first workshop here. She's a teacher, and she's worked with

Alexis. She knows something about how to coordinate programs."

A few minutes later I turned and saw Marissa. It seemed like all my plans were simply forming on their own. All I had to do was talk, introduce people, and let things happen. In no time we had a meeting scheduled at my house between Marissa and Anthony's team. Maybe the EI agency didn't like Verbal Behavior, but that night the gods were smiling on it.

To cap things off, at the end of the evening I finally introduced myself to Alexis. Maybe I'd just needed a run of luck like that to take my shyness away. She looked at me and said: "Well, now I can put a face with all those emails. I hope you feel like these workshops are helping."

"Yes," I said. "You can't imagine how much they're helping."

CHAPTER OBSERVATIONS

There are still many areas of the country where Verbal Behavior methods simply aren't known. Therapists and programmers may be willing to learn about them, but where are they supposed to turn? This is where individuals can make a difference, but it will help if you know where to look.

One excellent source of all the information you'll need to learn more about Verbal Behavior is: www.christinaburke.com/GettingStarted.htm. This site lists different organizations, videos, and websites where you can contact professionals about setting up a program or workshop.

The following videos can help in learning more about Verbal Behavior. They act as introductions, and provide the tools for understanding these methods:

- ☐ Carbone CD Seminar Set by Dr. Vincent J. Carbone, available at www.abatoolchest.com.

- "Teaching Verbal Behavior: An Introduction to Parents Teaching Language" by Dr. James Partington, available at Behavior Analysts, Inc. www.behavioranalysts.com, and Different Roads to Learning, www.difflearn.com.
- The Early Learner at Home, available at www.autism.teachingtools.com.
- Evy's Progress by Autism Teaching Tools™, available at www.autism.teachingtools.com.

At the following websites you should be able to find pertinent information about setting up workshops in your area:

- Information at www.drcarbone.net.
- Workshops by Christina Burk, information at www.christinaburkaba.com.
- Information at www.verbalbehaviornetwork.com for workshops and outreach.
- Workshops and outreach listings at www.poac.net (Parents of Autistic Children)..
- Information about Verbal Behavior Training at www.vbntraining.com

CHAPTER TWELVE

We scheduled the meeting between Marissa and Anthony's therapists for the middle of March. Just having a date for it excited me. I was so ready for this change. For almost a year my hopes for Verbal Behavior had been just that: hopes. We had all talked a lot, and we'd tried a few things that we could figure out from reading, but the more we did the more obvious it had become that partial approaches didn't work. Anthony needed the whole VB method.

When the night of the big meeting came Marissa arrived early.

"I was hoping I could talk to you before anyone else gets here."

"Sure," I said. I was glad for the chance.

"Show me his programs, and tell me what you've done so far with VB."

"Really, just some manding," I said, and I described everything we had tried. "It's not much," I concluded.

"Still it's worthwhile," she said. "None of it can hurt with Anthony, and the fact that you've gotten the therapists into it helps put all of you on the same page. So you're ready now?"

"As ready as I'm going to be," I said. "I really am completely committed to giving Verbal Behavior a chance. I'm tired of hearing people who aren't here every day telling me how much he's progressing. They look at the book, and see things on paper, but it's all that they want to see. His therapists know. They're here every day. They'll tell you."

She nodded. "I realize that it's the people who are with him constantly who can give me the most meaningful feedback. I'm not just going to be looking at progress reports."

"I know you're not," I said.

"We'll put the books aside," she told me.

I was thinking about how glad I was to hear those words when Anthony's team showed up. Susan and Stacy spent the most time with Anthony, so they did most of the talking. Marissa had questions for us, and we all had a whole lot of questions for her.

"If we're going to do this right we're going to have to stop the trials completely," Marissa told us.

I could see a sudden fear in the therapists' eyes. Their fear must have been contagious, because I felt a sudden pang of it myself. I wanted this, but suddenly I could clearly see how wide the gulf was between what we had been doing, and what was to come.

"Completely?" I asked, voicing their question for them.

Marissa looked down at her notes, then up at us. "This isn't something we can do halfway. Also, it's not like an addiction on Anthony's part. We aren't trying to wean him off something that his body and mind need or crave. Anthony has things in his life, some positive, some negative, some neutral.

"The most important positives he has are you, the people who are with him every day. He knows you care about him, and he has a sense that you do what you do to help him. But from the record it's clear that he doesn't much like trialing. Maybe it's not hurting him. Maybe it's neutral in terms of what it is, but to him it's just another thing he puts up with each day. When he points at something, or when he shows you he's caught on to some sound, picture, or gesture, he's just trying to get it over with. So to him it's almost certainly a negative.

"I'm hoping VB will be a positive. I think he'll like the VB methods. A lot of kids do. You've already tried some of it with him, and he does okay with a lot of it. He doesn't cry the minute you prompt him to mand for something. So let's get rid of the methods he sees as negatives, and start on something that he might just come to enjoy—something that can be a positive. If we were to mix the two he might just start out with the same attitudes and ideas about VB that he has about trialing."

"But don't we need to know more?" Susan asked.

"Sure, but you already know a lot, and you'll learn the rest. You'll learn a lot just doing it with him."

They still looked a little doubtful. "Guys," I said, "what if we try it for a month? If he doesn't make any progress we can always go back to the trials."

"But what if he loses the skills he's already got?" Susan asked. "After all, he's learned some things from trialing."

"He has learned some things," said Marissa, "and those skills are important. But until Anthony is manding consistently and spontaneously he won't really have full use of any of those skills. He won't forget what you've taught him. He'll just develop a much larger skill set to plug those things into. Anthony is two years and three months. He should be pairing and manding, and he can." She turned to me. "What do you think, Chris?"

"I think he can, if we all help him," I said.

Then Marissa started going through some details. This helped. It was much easier for us all to accept the changes when they became concrete. "We'll start with pairing and some target mands," Marissa said. "We're going to need counters, some erasable boards, and we'll need some kind of setup where we can easily give him what he wants or needs, but where none of it is in his reach."

She went on about the hows, whats, and whys, but one of the most important changes to me was setting aside that big red trial book. I was happy to throw that thing in a drawer.

Anthony had already mastered music, jump, cookie, milk and water, so we decided to start our target mands with ball, book, bubble, TV and car. We put dry erase boards on the wall. On these we wrote the mands: ones he'd mastered, and ones we were targeting. That way any of us could glance at the wall, and see what we should be working on. We all got counters to keep track of the number of mands, and data sheets so we could record the number of mands per minute.

Before any of these things could be effective Anthony's therapists needed to pair with him. "Pairing" sounds like something that would already be done after a year of therapy, but this had to be done in such a way that the new methods would make sense. Anthony had to see the connection between himself and the therapist, and then he could learn the connection between her and the thing he wanted. This pairing was a crucial step to a successful program.

I bought a cheap armoire and used it to sanitize the environment in the room where Anthony got his therapy. This involved putting almost everything he wanted out of reach. What didn't fit in the armoire went into clear Rubbermaid bins. Now he would have to communicate to get his wants and needs. Everything else I put in clearly marked Rubbermaid bins. I left a few things out and accessible to him.

Up until now Anthony had liked his therapists, but he also saw them as people who placed a lot of demands on him. Whenever they arrived he knew he would have to work. "Pairing" promised to change that dynamic, helping him bond with them in a whole new way.

"Now he's going to see you as big chocolate chip cookies," Marissa told them.

"Really?" Stacy asked.

"Sure. You'll be conditioned reinforcers, but that translates into something he likes. That's because whenever he mands you'll be able to give him something he wants."

Marissa set up dates to come and work with each therapist during sessions with Anthony. We videotaped some sessions to send to Marissa so she could evaluate how things were working. This may sound intrusive, but it wasn't. That's because this therapy allowed for some leeway.

We all understood that we would make some mistakes, and that was built into the program. Anthony would be changing, so we would have to be changing too. If we made mistakes, we learned from them. Sometimes the thing that worked yesterday no longer works today. Often that meant that Anthony had reached some other level, which showed us that we must change our own behavior according to the child. Now we were back to that Doug Grier quote that I'd heard almost a year before: "Be a strategic scientist." With Anthony we were becoming a team of strategic scientists.

By the end of March Anthony's therapists had really begun to pair with him, and they were looking for strong reinforcers to act as supports for this. They worked creatively, looking for the things he liked best. Among his favorites were snacks, like chips and brownies, and playful stuff like swings and tickling.

Now it was time to bring in the family. We began incorporating Austin and Daniella into the sessions. In a way this was more a matter of Anthony's life entering into that of the family than the other way around. Through the past year when the therapist had come, he and the therapist would go into his room and shut the door. Two hours later they would come out, and Anthony would reenter our larger, family world.

That separation didn't need to be there; it wasn't even desirable. From now on the sessions would spread throughout our house. This was the environment he lived in, so he would have to develop and use his skills throughout this area. It was a little like an aviator moving off the flight simulator, and getting behind the controls of a real plane. Anthony had to learn to fly.

When I'd introduced the dietary changes, and later brought in the methyl B12, Anthony had become more aware of his brother and sister. With this awareness came interest, but still there was a separation simply because he couldn't communicate the same way they could. Now we started pairing Austin and Daniella with reinforcers. We got them to hand him things he loved. Along with this we started playing group games like duck-duck-goose or hide-n-seek.

On April 10, 2004 during the second week of our formal VB Program we started keeping good data on the manding. The team had developed targets that they were teaching Anthony to request. He wasn't verbal yet, so he did these mands in sign language. They spent each two-hour session going through the process of motivating him for something, and then as he reached for it, prompting him to mand for it. As he learned his therapists faded the prompts. Anthony took to it well, and after his therapists left, I followed up, getting him to mand all day.

This was the way to make what he was learning stick with him. If a kid gets two hours a day of something from people who are only there during that time, he may only associate it with that time and setting. In VB the family should be the main therapists, carrying the therapy into day-to-day life. Everyone has to get involved.

This sounds terribly demanding, but it isn't as hard as it sounds. After all, even a child of four or five like Daniella can understand what manding is all about. It's just asking for something. If he asks for something, and if he's allowed to have it, you give it to him. Soon Daniella was manding with Anthony all the time. It shouldn't be too surprising that she picked up on the process all by herself.

Meal and bath times proved to be great opportunities. These are times when there are many different things that they want, and that you can give them, one after another. Also, one request will relate to the next. At the table one food often relates to another (think bread-and-butter). In the bath a child might have one floating toy that fits with another (two boats, or two animals). These relationships soon work into ideas about generalizing, and a child begins to see that mealtimes encompass a group of particular things, while baths take in a different set of items, yet the same process works with both. As they request and relate, these linkages will form in their minds. The more you hit the mands the quicker they will pick this up and generalize.

We all worked with Anthony to the point where hardly a waking hour went by without many mands, and many responses. As he related various items and actions into groups we could see him starting to put his world together in ways that were immediately useful to him. He liked this. It was soon clear that Anthony was much happier doing VB. He was motivated in a way that he'd never been before. He became a manding machine. As soon as I would come in from work he would run to me and sign for "bubble." The first time this happened I was shocked. The bubbles were nowhere to be seen. He wasn't playing with them. He simply knew that I would be able to get him the bubbles, so as soon as he saw me he asked for them. When a child mands for something, you want to reinforce it immediately, so there I was, rummaging through my drawers to find the bubbles. I found them, and began blowing them. He manded to pop them, this time vocally! "Wow," I said out loud.

This happened every day. It quickly changed from bubbles, to toys, to whatever it was he was thinking of as I came in the door. He did it other times too—all the time—and more and more he was replacing signs with sounds: he was beginning to figure out words. This happened within weeks.

By May this was happening a lot. One day when Susan was holding him he reached for me. I started to take him, but she said: "Wait Chris. He wants you, so let's see if he'll mand for you." He reached again. Susan said: "Ma, ma."

Anthony answered: "Ba ba."

"Yay!" she cheered, handing him to me.

I held him and hugged him for a few seconds. She took him back. He reached out to me. Susan repeated: "Ma ma."

"Ba ba."

She gave him to me again. I handed him back he chirped: "Ba ba." She handed him right back to me. We kept going with it, and it seemed like we could go on forever. This was one he had down.

The next day was Mother's Day. All day Anthony kept saying: "Ba ba," for me. I called Susan, crying. "Thank you, Susan. This is the best Mother's Day ever!"

It wasn't long before "Ba ba" became "Ma ma" and this quickly morphed into "Mommy." For a year we'd been trying to teach him 'Mommy." The therapists had gone so far as the build a little shrine with my picture in the therapy room, getting him to point at it. He'd known the picture was called "Mommy", but he'd never said it, and never transferred the idea of the picture to me. Now, to my son, I had a name.

Anthony soon had about fifteen to twenty mands down. As he reached this level he started manding consistently, being able to crossover from one environment to another, and one person to another. I wasn't the only one he asked for bubbles, and he didn't just ask for them when he saw me come in the door.

Once he reached this level it was time for us to move on to Natural Environment Teaching (NET). NET involves teaching a child skills in his or her natural environment. For instance we would start with a toy animal farm. As we began playing with Anthony we would place specific kinds of demands so that he could learn how language worked. These were called Verbal Operants. There were *receptive* verbal operants, such as, "Get the pig," then there were operants called *tacting* or labeling such as holding up the pig and saying: "What is this?" If the child responds, "Pig" then he just labeled or tacted the pig. A third kind of verbal operant was *intraverbal*, talking about something that's not there, such as the pig when it's out of sight. You might say: "The pig says..." then wait for the child to say: "Oink." You incorporate the targeted skills with the activity or toy, and you always keep the child manding. Manding is a verbal operant as well.

At this point that seemed to be the eleventh commandment: Always keep Anthony manding. This was getting easier and easier to do. He manded so often on his own, that sometimes I hardly noticed.

CHAPTER OBSERVATIONS

You can find the counters you need for manding at office supply stores such as Staples or Office Depot or at sporting goods stores. They also sell them at www.difflearn.com. The mands become so frequent that the counter becomes the best way to keep accurate figures. You really need to know the numbers, because it could go up or down a lot without you being sure what's happening. If you keep the counter in your pocket or around your neck, you can always count the mands.

Video taping is a key method in making sure everyone is consistent with teaching procedures. The tapes help to analyze the actions and progress of therapists and therapy, as well as the child. If everyone watches the tapes, each of you can see small areas where something might be falling out of synch. This helps keep a uniform approach to manding and other areas. It also helps everyone concerned to avoid the trap of blaming the child. In VB if the child is not responding, most likely the error is in the therapy and teaching, not in the child. Tapes will help identify the precise problem. I taped several sessions of myself working with Anthony. As I would watch myself I was always amazed at the things I'd missed or mistakes I'd made.

Pairing needs creative approaches. Take something the child loves. An example might be Sponge Bob. Use this as a reinforcer to get him interested in other activities. Take the Sponge Bob action figure, put it on a toy train and have Sponge Bob riding around to lead the child into the new activity of trains. Draw Sponge Bob or paint a picture of him to get the child interested in painting or drawing. Pair the thing they like to something they haven't experienced yet. The connections don't always have to be obviously logical. They only need to be possible in terms of the toys and activities.

Karen, one of Rocco's therapists knew he had a thing for license plates. He loved any car license plate. When Rocco needed some strong reinforcers at school Karen got images off the net, and printed out images of fifteen license plates. Soon she had Rocco making license plates out of gluten-free Play Doh. Now Rocco loves working with play doh.

One of the best ways to see NET is as the mand sandwich. Mand, add skills, and mand more. For example Anthony would mand for the farm animals, so we could eventually teach more verbal operants with them. Keep the skills easy at first, prompting the answer. Fade in the number of demands slowly. You can take the same targeted skills, such as those learned with farm animals, then have the child learn the same skills in terms of the farm house, or coloring pictures of farms, or making a clay model of a farm. Soon you might get a computer game involving a farm. This way you expand the child's skills, and their ability to apply the skills to any situation that needs them.

Be creative, think outside of the box. Susan and Stacy would make lesson plans for NET, writing down all the questions they could ask him on an index card, then placing it in the toy. This helped us a lot. If we thought of a new question we would add it to the index card. With each toy you might have a cheat sheet listing the target skills that go with the toy, and different ways to ask about them. This way you help one another, with everyone sharing every great idea.

This made it easy for me. At any time I could pull out the farm house and find an index card with pertinent questions—often ones I'd never seen before. I wasn't always forced to think up a new question. With this kind of practice you get better at thinking up new questions of your own.

Using NET data sheets, you can probe the child, figuring out which skills need work prior to each session. With Anthony the sessions concentrated on pairing, manding and natural environment teaching.

Many programs add carrier phrases such as "I want____" or "Can I have____." This is good, but some programs add this too early. The child only knows five requests, then gets hit with this. At such an early point it makes talking even harder. Alexis suggests keeping the one word mand until they have at least 50-to-75 separate one word requests. If you wait until then to bring in carrier phrases, then the child will be fluent enough with the whole process of manding to make the jump, and you'll soon have 50-to-75 sentences.

CHAPTER THIRTEEN

Navigating through all the difficulties of raising and helping an autistic child is never easy. After the smooth sailing of the last couple of chapters, I should remind you of that. The days of progress are beautiful, and any progress, large or small, outweighs all disappointments, but you must be ready for troubling moments, and even bad days, weeks and months.

I include this story here because I know it will be balanced by the ongoing chronicle of Anthony's progress through that spring. It happened at about the same time. In the last chapter we were covering mid-March to May of 2004. Now I will backtrack slightly to March 10, 2004.

When you have a two-year-old like Anthony you are already thinking past the therapy at home, and considering whatever choices are available for schools in your area. I had to be concerned about this because Anthony would go past the age of eligibility for Early Intervention programs before the end of the year. I wanted a preschool. I had been visiting different ones in our county, hoping to find a good Verbal Behavior program. I was excited to hear of a program in the next town over, and I had made an appointment to observe a class there.

I had read about this preschool, talked to them on the phone, and I'd heard a little buzz here and there. According to what I'd heard this school was closely adhering to Skinner's analysis of Verbal Behavior, and its applications to the education of autistic children, and children with other learning disorders.

What I found was a school where children were being turned into robots. There were snacks set out everywhere, with no attention whatsoever to a child's individual dietary needs. Most of the food was stuff Anthony couldn't eat without suffering the kind of setback he'd had after the milk episode. To make matters worse, crumbs were everywhere. In my mind's eye I saw Anthony picking up scraps off the floor and eating them.

The crumbs and general disarray seemed to be an accurate reflection of the attitude of the staff. The teachers seemed overwhelmed, and their aides had the look of newcomers who had been forced into service.

I felt horribly let down. From what people had said to me, and in my phone conversations with people at the school this had seemed like a real possibility—a program nearby where Anthony could begin his school career. It was a decision that was so completely dictated by his autism, and by the therapy and diet we had put together for him. A program that actually practiced VB had seemed to hold such promise. I hadn't expected perfection, and if the food had been the lone problem I would've have looked for a way to fight that battle—to point out to administrators enlightened enough to have VB that diet was just as important. Battles like that might be winnable, but what I was seeing was a school that had lost the war.

I went out, got in my car, and faced the afternoon traffic. "What now?" I thought.

To this was added the grayness of late winter, and a March day that wouldn't let go of the cold. I felt a shiver welling up from my stomach. Keep in mind: though this was partway into Alexis's workshops, we hadn't had the meeting with Marissa yet. Anthony had improved after Christmas with the methyl B12 shots, but at that moment we'd reached a plateau, and we had been on those before. School was a huge empty place up ahead. It might be full of promise, or it might be the biggest threat yet. What I had just seen seemed designed to undo every bit of progress we'd made. I saw my son eating crumbs off the floor, then slowly sitting down among them, the blankness filling his eyes as his mouth fell open.

At home my dad was babysitting. When I get there he looked at me. "Are you okay?" he asked.

"I'm fine," I said. "It was just that school. They don't know what they're doing."

"I'm sorry, Chris. Don't worry. You'll find something." He told me what was happening there on the home front, then he went out the door.

I stood there, feeling distracted and shaky as I sorted through the mail. There was another packet from Dr. Neubrander. Normally I looked forward to these as challenges. There was always more to do, but I could usually see that as a sign that we were progressing. But that day I tore open the envelope, and began to read, then suddenly felt as if the air around me was getting heavier. Each new instruction was added weight in an intolerable burden. There were dozens of new supplements. I would have to break each capsule into different amounts to get the appropriate dosage. Each dose seemed to have a different schedule.

"How will I ever do this every day?" I whispered. The list fell from my hands. I looked up, and the room started spinning.

Suddenly the kids were screaming. I felt a huge bubble of rage rising up in me. "I need quiet!" I shouted. "Be quiet! Now!"

I looked down. Daniella was staring up at me, her eyes frightened. I knew I must have looked like a monster. I grabbed the phone and punched my dad's cell number. As soon as I heard his voice I cried: "Dad, please, come back and get the kids!"

"Honey, what's wrong?"

I made a strained effort to calm myself. "Don't ask, Dad. Please, just do it!"

"I'm coming," he said.

I started pacing around the room. I couldn't think straight. I felt like I was about to vomit. Two minutes later Dad walked in. He didn't ask questions. He looked as if he was afraid too.

"I'll take the kids," he said.

A minute later they were all going out the door.

In the kitchen I slipped down slowly, then curled up on the floor. I sobbed: "No, please, God," I whispered. "I can't do this anymore..."

It took a few minutes to get enough control to make another call. I wanted my husband, Don. I was still there on the kitchen floor. As soon as I'd punched his work number I felt the hysteria taking hold of me again.

On the other end of the line I heard Don's voice.

"Don!" I cried. "Help me, I can't do this... I can't..."

For a moment I heard nothing, then he said: "Where are the kids, Chris?"

"My dad has them. Please help me."

"It's okay, hon. We'll be okay." His voice sounded shaky in my ear.

"Don, I need to go to the hospital. Please take me to the hospital."

"Stay on the phone with me, Chris. Don't hang up."

That phone call seemed like only minutes, but later I learned it had lasted an hour. Don was far too frightened of what might happen to hang up. He wanted to come home, but he couldn't hang up, not even for a few minutes. He knew I was having a nervous breakdown. I later realized that I had probably blacked out a lot of our conversation. I'd been talking without even knowing what I was saying, and none of that stayed in my memory anymore than the million separate details of a bad dream.

That night my cousins, Sharon and Kimmy, came over. "We want you to go to the doctor," said Sharon.

"I don't know," I said. I wasn't protesting. I was simply exhausted, and couldn't imagine doing anything.

"We do," said Kimmy. "Come on."

I went with them.

The doctor listened to all that had happened (or all any of us knew), and prescribed an anti-depressant. As they drove me home I felt drained.

In the morning I felt a little better, and it was only a few days after that when we met with Marissa. By that time I'd found my optimism again, school or no school.

I share this story with you as a reminder that this is not an easy road. You spend each day teetering between hope and disaster. You want nothing more than a normal life for your child, yet that desire is greater than anything you have ever felt. And it seems so unfair sometimes. All the other children—other peoples' and your own—have their chance to take their place in the world, and become independent people. For them it seems ready-made. And then there is this little boy or girl with a mysterious illness threatening to steal them away, leaving an empty shell of a child, seemingly incapable of any meaningful thought or action.

It's not fair. It gets to you. If it didn't you wouldn't be human. And you may need some extra help from a professional. That's okay.

Some of us don't accept help easily. That was me. I was the one who could handle it all—until I crashed. Then I was too exhausted to understand what had happened to me. Luckily I had people who cared. I let them lead me to the doctor. I took my prescription. It helped me focus. It took the constant lump out of my throat and the knot out of my stomach.

Thank God, that never happened again!

***

By late April my breakdown was a memory. That's not to say that there weren't rough spots. The struggle against autism is never easy, and then there are all the normal bumps in the road, the kind that face any little boy at two-and-a-half. But now Anthony's VB therapy was in place, and the whole EI team could see that we'd made the right choice.

With Verbal Behavior methods Anthony excelled. All of us watched as this blossoming little guy learned more in a few weeks than he had in a year of mass trialing. Those ABA methods were like useless, broken old toys in the back of a closet, so beat up you couldn't even give them away. The trialing notebook stayed in the drawer, a forgotten record of standing still.

It wasn't just the Verbal Behavior therapy. Anthony's rapid progress was due to a two-pronged approach: biomedical and VB. Neither would have been half as effective without the other. This was a case of synergy. In the past sixteen months Don and I had seen how each alteration in diet affected our son. We had watched him improve with the removal of dairy products from his diet. We had seen how cutting out gluten, and targeting areas like carbohydrates could affect him. Finally, we had marched to the drumbeat of Dr. Neubrander's instructions, using supplements to target various problems, then starting him on the methyl B12shots.

These steps had combined to make Anthony happier, healthier and more engaged. Finally he had the focus necessary to take interest in the world around him. One could see his horizons expand from the ends of his fingertips out into the room, and beyond to the whole house. He even knew there was a world outside, and that there were some fun things out there. It was like layers of fog lifting.

Not that his health was perfect. For instance, Anthony's bowels continued to be a problem, and he was often dependent on Miralax or Senna to have a bowel movement. Difficulties like these reminded me that we were still climbing a mountain, and though the summit was closer, we still had a long way to go.

Still, all of us could see that with his healthier body, Anthony was far more able to take advantage of his new therapy. As we began the process of systematically pairing and manding, Anthony was ready for us. He quickly learned signals and sounds that conveyed his wants and needs. More than ever I was seeing my son emerge from the darkness into the world at large.

It was in this context that I attended the next DAN conference. This was the big one, and they were holding it outside Washington, D.C. just a five-hour drive from my home. I wanted to see a truly big DAN conference. I wanted to meet the authors of the books I'd been reading, and talk to them about my son's ongoing recovery. I wanted to listen to every word they said.

I hoped my friend, Laura, would go with me. She wanted to but hesitated. Her daughter, Francesca was still an infant, and she wasn't sure about leaving her husband, Rob, alone to take care of Rocco and their new daughter.

"Go," Rob told her.

"Are you sure?" she asked.

"Of course I'm sure," he said. "I can take care of them for a couple of days, and you need to learn everything you can to help Rocco."

"And you know what to do?" she asked.

"Sure. We'll be fine," he said.

We packed up the truck in the early morning. It wasn't just us going. My parents and Austin were coming along too. My dad wanted to hear the speakers. He'd made Anthony's autism into a personal project, reading all he could about it. This was his chance to learn more.

My mom was going to make the trip into a mini-vacation with her grandson, Austin. While we got all we could out of the conference, my mom and Austin would go sightseeing in the District. Don stayed home with Daniella and Anthony. My only worry there was my two youngest kids were staying home with the biggest kid in the house. It wasn't much of a worry. I knew they could use a weekend on their own.

We arrived at the hotel around dinner time. My dad said to Laura and me: "Why don't you two have dinner here. We'll take Austin somewhere where we can have some fun. That way you two can relax, and maybe see some of these authors you've got me reading."

"Thanks, Dad," I said, giving him a hug.

Laura and I were glad to have a quiet dinner there at the hotel, then we walked around, looking at the setup. The conference took up most of the hotel's main floor. There were three ballrooms off a large hallway. People and organizations had put up booths in the hallway where you could get information on all the various ideas about fighting autism. There would be speeches and presentations in the ballrooms. One of the ballrooms was being set up for a large dinner. We'd heard about that, though we hadn't signed up for it.

Laura and I walked around looking at the various booths. I was amazed at the physical proximity of so many companies and organizations that I had only experienced on the Internet. Laura and I weren't the only ones poking about. We found other parents doing the same thing. We were all hungry for information—anything that could help us get to the next step.

As I stood among these people I found myself feeling comfortable in a way I had almost forgotten. So often this past year I had felt out of place. Because this sense of dislocation never left me, it had reached a point where I barely noticed it. Yet it was always a factor. I would be standing at the bus stop overhearing neighbors talking about school, or I might be listening to people in my family talking about an upcoming birthday, and suddenly I would feel disconnected. I'd be envious of little problems: a bad mark on a quiz, or what birthday gift to buy-- I could barely relate to those things. "Don't they know how blessed they are?" I would think. "Don't they realize how lucky it is to have a child who can express happiness, sadness, pleasure and pain?" Of course they didn't. That was their blessing and their luck, but it became hard for me to see. I had to worry about mixing up 40 supplements in the right proportions. I had to think about whether this was the day for an injection. Could I mimic this cookie or that using rice flour? What did I do when the health food store was out of Anthony's favorite chips? And what about that next manding opportunity? Didn't I need to be ready for that as soon as I turned around?

I had two beautifully normal kids, and my worries about them seemed so minimal. Was that right? Was I paying enough attention? I didn't know. There were so many things I didn't know, but I was always sure of this: I had this little boy with sparkly brown eyes and big cheeks who was counting on me!

There in the hotel, wandering among the booths with all those other parents, suddenly I wasn't disconnected. For the first time in almost two years I fit right in. The mom next to me knew what chelation was. That dad over there had a pretty good notion of what methylcobalomin was. They knew who Dr. Bernard Rhimland was, and they knew that DAN stood for "Defeat Autism Now." They were on my planet!

Laura joined me, and she and I walked around star struck. We kept pulling on each other's shirts.

"Hey, is that Jacqlyn McCandless?"

"Oh, look there's Stephanie Cave."

"We've got to find Lisa Lewis."

"And Karyn Serousi."

These last two had founded ANDI. When we returned to our room Laura called the front desk and asked to be connected to Karyn Serousi's room. Karyn answered.

Laura introduced herself. "Your book changed my life," Laura gushed.

"I'm so glad," Karyn replied. "Are you going to be at the dinner party?"

"We're getting ready for it now," Laura said, "though we're just going to stop by. We didn't sign up for it."

"It doesn't matter if you didn't sign up," Karyn said. "Anyone's welcome to stop in for as long as they like. Look for me there. I'd love to meet both of you in person."

When we were ready we took the elevator downstairs, and went to the ballroom where they were having the dinner. It wasn't formal, though people were dressed nicely. It was in the largest ballroom, and there must have been 500 people, some sitting at tables, while others mingled. Laura and I got drinks, then walked around. The dinner party featured several motivational speakers including one by Maureen McDonnell who had helped Anthony and me get ready for Dr. Neurbrander's treatments. Dr. Sidney Baker spoke, welcoming everyone there, and giving us the sense of being together in this struggle for our children's brains and bodies. Both of them spoke to our hearts, always holding out the prospect of hope for every autistic child. Once again, among all of these people who dealt with the same problems I did, I felt a feeling of belonging that I had sorely missed. But it wasn't just warm feelings and uplifting speeches. Now we were talking to the authors whose words had inspired us so much.

Then we ran into Dr. Neubrander. "I'm glad to see parents here," he said. "So often these things are only the professionals, but I think it's good for us to have you, the patients' parents, here to check on us. After all, you're the ones there with the children every day."

"I'm just enjoying being here," I said. "So many people who deal with the same things I do."

"That's what I'm talking about," Dr. Neubrander agreed.

Finally we realized we'd had a long day. We were more tired than we realized, and we wanted to be fresh in the morning, so we called it an evening. That wasn't as easy as it sounds. We were tempted to stay and talk to these people for hours longer.

In the morning, the first speaker was Elaine Gottschall. Already in her eighties, Elaine (who, sadly, has since passed away) was a great proponent of the SCD diet. Her lecture that morning was titled: "The Gut-Brain-Diet Connection: the Specific Carbohydrate Diet."

Though I didn't realize it when she started, her speech would have a huge impact on my own thinking about Anthony's diet. In the space of a single hour Elaine showed me a whole new approach that made sense to me.

I had heard of the Specific Carbohydrate Diet, and I'd gone so far as to do a little research about it on the Internet. But then I saw casein in the foods, and that turned me off. I had already gone to the gluten-free-casein-free (GFCF) diet, and I liked the results. I wasn't about to reintroduce something that I'd come to think of as a negative.

But there I sat in the audience, listening to a mother of an autistic child who was introducing Elaine. This woman's son had suffered terrible bowel problems. This made me think of Anthony's lingering difficulties with his bowels. I listened as this woman gave an account of her son's severe pain. Despite a good doctor, steroids, and a strict GFCF diet, the boy's problems persisted. His doctor came to the point of having to cut off the boy's prednisone, and was at a loss on what to do next. "I became desperate," the mother told us. "In his pain my boy was beginning to hurt himself. I felt like driving us both off the nearest bridge. I'd read Elaine's book over a year earlier, but I'd never tried the diet she described. I did remember it though, and finally I pulled the book off the shelf, and tried it. By that time I was ready for one last chance. That was when my son's pain began to fade. He stopped trying to hurt himself, and every day he looked and acted healthier. I watched this miracle happen, and to this day I know what did it: the Specific Carbohydrate Diet."

With that she introduced Elaine Gottschall.

Elaine followed, showing us her non-nonsense approach, fueled by a generous passion. We could feel her courage, strength, and her sense of fun too. This was the first time she'd been asked to speak at a DAN conference, and she was going to make the most of it. She was there to preach to all of us who used the GFCF approach; she was there to change our minds, and our children's diets. She was determined to convert us to the SCD. She used logic to force us to question a diet that wouldn't allow our children to eat fruit due to the sugar, yet loaded them with potatoes and rice. "What are potatoes and rice?" she asked. "Starches. And what do starches turn into? Sugar! Bad sugar! That's what they turn into in your child's body."

I looked around the room. Most of these parents had gone to great trouble to get their autistic kids on the GFCF diet. Just outside the ballroom doors vendors setting up booths to sell us rice cookies, potato milk and other GFCF staples. There were baskets for a Chinese auction and their contents were nothing but rice and potato products. Yet here was this elderly woman essentially saying: All of you are wrong.

I get impressed by courage and logic. This woman had both. She certainly had my attention. She obviously knew a lot about the gut, so I wanted to hear her reasoning. I don't know if talk about starches and digestion gets you going, but I was on the edge of my seat. I listened as she made her case for the Specific Carbohydrate Diet (SCD).

Nearly half a century before Elaine had faced the scary road of healing an ill child. Her eight-year-old daughter, Judy, had severe ulcerative colitis. Elaine searched out the medical approaches of the day, but they were unsuccessful. It looked as if Judy would have to undergo surgery to remove part of her intestines. Elaine heard of a doctor in New York City, Sidney Valentine Haas. Dr.Haas put Judy on the Specific Carbohydrate Diet. The changes came within days. Judy's symptoms were completely gone within two years. She grew up to live a healthy life.

The science behind this diet intrigued Elaine. She wasn't used to the idea of a diet that could cure an otherwise incurable disease. The experience inspired her to study nutrition and biology. After receiving a bachelor's degree from Montclair State College, Elaine joined the Department of Cell Science at the University of Western Ontario's Zoology Department. She earned her Master's while studying the effects of sugars on the digestive tract. In 1980, when she was nearly 60 years old, Elaine began investigating changes that occur in the intestinal wall during inflammatory bowel disease.

There at the DAN conference Elaine explained bowel disease in great detail, and how this related to the SCD diet. She told us how different foods affect the digestive system in different ways, and how this is particularly true of sugars. The complex carbohydrates of the rice, potatoes and other starches in the GFCF diet can exacerbate symptoms. Since these foods just keep coming, without a break, the diet creates the symptoms, and then goes on feeding them. It's the classic vicious cycle. The SCD diet was devised primarily to treat conditions stemming from Crohn's Disease, Ulcerative Colitis, Inflammatory Bowel Syndrome, and Celiac Disease, but with so many autistic children having similar bowel disorders it made sense that it could help. Elaine had seen the diet work for many autistic kids.

When Elaine's speech ended Laura and I looked at each other.

"Are you thinking what I'm thinking?" I asked her.

"We have to try this," she said.

I nodded. "I can't stand it, but she makes sense. And here, I was finally used to the whole GFCF thing."

"I know what you mean," Laura said.

"I know where to get the snacks he likes..."

"What he can have or not have," Laura said, thinking of her own son.

"Almost everything they eat has rice or potato in it," I said.

"Do you really think we should change?" Laura asked me.

"I think we should try it," I said. "Anthony's bowels are still pretty bad."

Laura nodded. "Rocco's too."

If the two of us sound as if we were easily swayed by a single speech, you have to remember that last thing: we both had boys who, despite all their other progress, were still having persistent, serious bowel issues. We were both still searching for a cure. While the GFCF diet removes the drugging effect on the brain, decreasing many cognitive, sensory and behavioral symptoms, it doesn't heal the gut. What we were hearing was the promise of a diet that could do that, while addressing those other problems as well. The news overwhelmed us only because we had done so much to commit ourselves to GFCF. But one principle that a parent must follow is to always look for improvement. Discipline is important in any diet or therapy, but an excess of rigidity is not. Elaine had both experience and logic on her side. We could try SCD and see if it worked. Also, we could do it together, comparing notes, and learning from each other.

At any DAN conference you are likely to come away with some huge new thing you have learned. Exactly what that thing is will depend on what stage you and your child have reached, and on who is speaking about what. For Laura and me at that conference it was the Specific Carbohydrate Diet. SCD would benefit both of our sons in the months and years to come.

But Elaine's revelations weren't the only high point. Throughout the weekend Laura and I learned so much. Naturally my dad took some time to walk through the booths, and listen to some speakers. He wasn't sorry. The whole experience deepened the knowledge he was already getting from his reading.

The second high point for Laura and me came on the conference's final day. The last presentation was given by Dr. Andy Wakefield. A veteran of the controversies that have swirled around the explosion of autism in the last fifteen years, Dr. Wakefield was one of the first to research the role of vaccines and mercury on the increase. Originally from England, he has published scores of articles and commentaries, and in 2001 he was awarded the Fellowship of the Royal College of Pathologists. He is medical advisor to the British charity, Visceral, and sits on the board of the United States charity, Medical Interventions for Autism.

Dr. Wakefield has stood on principle more than once, leaving the Royal Free School of Medicine rather than giving into pressures to limit his research. Now here he was at the DAN conference to give his side of that story. Cameras had come into the ballroom, signaling the presence of the media. Dr. Bernard Rhimland, who was introducing him, pointed out the cameras, saying to the parents in the audience: "If you have a child with autism, please stand." All of us who did stood. It was most of the audience. Then he said: "If you feel your child was damaged by the MMR vaccine, raise your hands, and wave to the cameras."

Laura has always been absolutely convinced that Rocco's autism began with this vaccine, just as I feel that the prime culprit with Anthony was antibiotics. Laura raised her hands, waving, her eyes filling with tears. I felt my own tears welling up as I supported her, holding her, and rubbing her back. Hundreds of parents swayed back and forth, crying just as we did.

At that moment that Dr. Rhimland introduced Dr. Andy Wakefield to the audience. This was a man who had given up a prominent career in England, leaving under fire, but not giving up the battle once he'd arrived in America.

In his speech Dr. Wakefield told us the details of what he had found, and the reaction that he'd met, and he thanked us for supporting him. His battle must have been terribly lonely, but now he knew he had allies. More and more people were listening, and many of us were beginning to do something about it, one child at a time.

It was an inspiring end to a conference that had moved everyone who had attended. Laura and I left with important new knowledge, and with a revitalized commitment to what we must do every day with our sons.

CHAPTER OBSERVATIONS

Lisa Lewis and Karyn Serousi founded the Autism Network for Dietary Intervention (ANDI). You can get more information at www.autismndi.com.

The following observations are a synthesis of my notes taken from Elaine Gottschall's speech, from further notes I made while reading her book, "Breaking the Vicious Cycle," as well as from other sources, and my own experiences with the workings of the SCD diet:

Different carbohydrates have different chemical structures. Understanding those differences, and what each carbohydrate does in the digestive tract, is the key to the SCD diet. The digestive system has good and bad bacteria. In a healthy intestinal tract they are in balance. These good and bad bugs fight for food, and this fighting should maintain the balance. People with bowel disease have a disturbance in that balance. Their guts have too much bad bacteria. If the bad bacteria outnumber the good then the bad get too much food and repopulate faster.

Food for bacteria lies in undigested particles, specifically those of carbohydrates. Typically you won't find bad bugs in the small intestine but if undigested carbohydrates pass into it the bad bacteria migrate there too. Undigested carbohydrates cause gas. Undigested carbohydrates in the small intestine increase the amount of gas there. Using fermentation the bad bugs in the gut go through their own digestion process. This produces toxins, making the gut's ph more acidic with lactic and acetic acids.

These acids corrode the intestinal wall, creating inflammation. The inflammation produces goblet cells which make mucus to protect the intestinal lining. The mucus covers the microvilli, which are the little fingers that stick out of the intestinal lining. These microvilli are like little hairs sticking out. They grab passing food particles and use enzymes to break them down so the food can be absorbed by the body. This breakdown is the essence of digestion. If these little hairs are covered by mucus they can't do their job.

The microvilli aren't the only things affected. The lymph nodes in the intestinal tract become swollen, much like the glands in your throat do when you are fighting a virus. This is the body's immune system reacting in a similar way in the gut. This reaction causes inflammation to flare up around the microvilli almost drowning them. With the microvilli out of commission you have even less chance of digesting complex carbohydrates.

These undigested carbohydrates are more food for the bad bacteria. All those bad bugs are having a party in your gut. They love carbohydrates, they love sugar, and now they have plenty of both. This produces more toxins causing more inflammation in the intestinal walls. Eventually the intestinal wall becomes ulcerated. Then the body puts extra water into the intestinal tract causing diarrhea. As this spirals out of control, a child feels pain, which often causes the bad dreams that we associate with stomach upsets.

SCD can bring this under control and help heal the gut. The diet must be strictly followed at all times to be effective. It is well-balanced and healthy consisting of whole, natural foods. Those health care professionals who oppose the diet usually do so on the basis of misinformation, or they simply don't think parents can, or will, do what is necessary to help their children strictly follow it. They don't have faith in us, so we must have faith in ourselves, and we must live up to that faith. This means that it's our responsibility to see that the diet is followed at all times, and in every situation. This sounds difficult, but remember: the rewards are great. Also, you have to consider the alternative: endless bowel problems, which means that much less progress overall.

SCD is a diet rich in the nutrition we all need. It excludes fast food, artificially colored imitation fruit snacks, juice boxes with only 10% juice the rest sugar, high sugar cereals, chips containing MSG and other harmful preservatives, cookies loaded with chemicals, and generally those highly processed foods that are chock full of additives. So what does that leave? A whole array of foods, including many whole fruits, vegetables, meat, poultry, eggs, fish, nuts and seeds.

One big concern parents voice when children go off dairy products is: where will the child get calcium? Plenty of foods are filled with calcium. I make Anthony's milk from almonds which are loaded with calcium. Tropicana Orange Juice has more calcium than milk. If you are worried there are calcium supplements.

There are answers similar to this one about every nutritional concern. This diet resembles what most healthy people ate prior to the age of processed foods, but it takes advantage of the variety of fresh foods and staples available in the modern age. The key advantage with SCD is that it is digestible. Its carbohydrates are in single molecule form called monosaccharides. These carbohydrates (sugars) can just be absorbed as is. They are found in fruits and honey.

The body absorbs monosaccharides without leaving food particles behind in the intestinal tract for the bad bacteria to feed on. You starve the bad bugs. Monosaccharide foods can be easily absorbed without more complex digestive processes. Byproducts and toxins decrease. The ph in the gut is adequate to neutralize acids. Inflammation subsides, giving the intestines a chance to heal.

The SCD diet avoids the multi-molecule (more complex) sugars: disaccharides and polysaccharides. These are the sugars that force the gut to work to break them down before they can be absorbed. An unhealthy gut won't break these down completely, and food will be left for the bad bacteria to feed on. That's when the bad bug party begins, and the bad bacteria thrive.

Examples of disaccharide-rich foods are milk, commercial yogurt, some supplements with lactose, table sugar, ketchup, canned foods, maltose, candy, and maple syrup. Examples of polysaccharide-rich foods are corn syrup, some vegetables, grain starch, and starches such as rice and potatoes. Both lists are almost endless.

Examples of monosaccharide sugars are glucose, fructose and galactose. Glucose and fructose are found in fruit, honey and some vegetables. Galactose is found in lactose-hydrolyzed milk and yogurt. Dairy can be a problem (it is with Anthony), but all you have to do is combine the SCD diet with a casein free diet, and add substitutes and supplements accordingly (as with the calcium cited above).

Elaine recommended doing a "starter diet" when beginning SCD. Typically this should be done for the first five days. Her book contains a recipe for a chicken soup that one can eat during this time. It is suggested for people with chronic diarrhea. She also recommends cooking your fruit in the early stages of the diet. There are other particulars, such as allowing bananas, but only when they are very ripe with black spots.

Elaine's website, www.breakingtheviciouscycle.com, has information about the SCD diet, including a legal and illegal list of foods.

The only sugar allowed on the SCD diet is honey. Fruit is also allowed, and can be added to recipes to give them a nice sweet flavor. Every kid will like different things, so experiment. Anthony loves strawberries, and bananas. He will try grapes and apples but they are not his favorite. Nut flours are allowed on the diet. I bake with almond flour, and it has a great flavor. Baking soda and all-natural vanilla are legal and great when baking. I cook with sunflower, safflower, and olive oils. A few of the foods that are NOT allowed on SCD are: baker's yeast, baking powder, barley, bologna, buckwheat, bulgur, buttermilk, carob, cereals, chick peas, chocolate, corn (and corn products), durum flour, cane juice, glucose candy, ketchup, maple syrup, marshmallow, millet, molasses, natural flavors, oats, pasta, pinto beans, rye, seed flour, soy products, Splenda, tapioca products, canned tomato products, wheat products, yams, and commercial yogurts.

Elaine also mentions the possibility of a regression at two to three months into the diet. This should be temporary and usually the child improves, with a leap in skills after the regression. This is due to a die-off of the yeast and bacteria in the gut. The child can become more aggressive and hyperactive, engaging in self-stimulatory behavior, tantrums, and/or spaciness. In some cases there may be some fever, and vomiting.

In some regressions the child could become more bloated, gassy, constipated and have more diarrhea. The child may also have the same regression symptoms as mentioned earlier, however this regression typically lasts two weeks and is also followed by a big improvement from the child. I remember Anthony going through a period of "sandy stool" at this time. I kept trying to figure out if he had somehow eaten sand. In my talks with other parents I have come to realize this is common.

Similar regressions are common at the five, seven, and nine month marks. These too are usually signs that the diet is working. Such regressions should only last from one to three weeks.

CHAPTER FOURTEEN

As soon as Laura and I got home we began to implement the SCD diet. My immediate goal was to see whether this diet could help me wean Anthony off the Senna supplement, and Miralax, the prescription laxative, both of which had been the main treatment for his bowel problems ever since December. Though both of these had helped, I hated the idea of Anthony being dependent on laxatives for the rest of his life. I wanted to see if there was some solution in the foods he ate every day.

Laura had exactly the opposite problem with Rocco. The worry with him was numerous bowel movements, and a lot of diarrhea. Could an SCD diet be the solution to both of our problems? We both had high hopes.

I gave Anthony a week to get used to the SDC diet. He seemed to take to it right away. He was less bloated, and I saw a difference in his stools—less mucous. Once a week had gone by I started slowly weaning him from the Miralax and Senna. I had tried this earlier in the spring without success. His constipation always returned. Now I carefully lowered the dosages of both, doing it as gradually as possible. Anthony remained regular. Finally, after about two weeks, he was off both the laxative and the supplement. Now he was going on his own every other day. His bowels were still soft but that wasn't a regression. From there his bowels kept improving. Within a couple of months Anthony was going daily. He finally had a formed stool, what Don and I called a "champion poop"-- no more mucus, no more straining, no more belly pain. If that had been the only improvement, I would have been sold on SCD, but this was a time when we were seeing a lot of advances. How much was the diet responsible for? I didn't know. I only knew that it was a vital component in our approach.

Laura's son, Rocco, was improving too. When she fed him the SCD diet Laura saw his stools hardening up. He didn't have as much diarrhea. Now we were both sold.

As part of our approach to Anthony's bowel problems, Dr. Neubrander wanted us to go to Dr.Krigsman, a gastroenterologist, who was going to do a colonoscopy. We were worried about the possibilities of autistic enterelcosis or other serious bowel conditions.

Two days of prep work preceded it—something Anthony couldn't understand. Part of it was not eating. He cried, pulling me toward the refrigerator. It's a mother's instinct to feed her child, and telling him "no" was one of the hardest things I ever did. The hours passed like eternity, as I watched my hungry, confused son wondering why I was doing this to him.

When the morning came to drive to Dr. Krigsman's office on Long Island, Anthony had a fever. We had to cancel. We rescheduled for July, but in the end Anthony's problems had cleared up to the point where we didn't do it at all. I was glad I didn't have to put Anthony through that again.

As of this writing (late 2006) Anthony is still on SCD, and I hope his diet will always consist of the kinds of natural foods the diet encourages. He has never had another problem with his bowel movements. This is the direct result of the SCD diet Elaine Gottschall recommended for autistic children across the board. I am thankful I heard her speak, and I urge parents of autistic children to heed what this great woman wrote. She is no longer with us, so we must all get the word out on the SCD diet.

In the months following the DAN Conference our efforts to fight Anthony's autism seemed to fit into a pattern and shape. Finally the treatments for his physical problems made sense in that they went along with the therapy for his brain. The SCD diet joined the methyl B12 injections and his supplements to bring Anthony back to the kind of physical health a little boy should have. All of this almost certainly helped with the Verbal Behavior methods. A healthy child is going to learn more readily than a sick child, no matter what. But if you have the right methods for both diet and learning, a child has the chance for real progress. Up until now Anthony had been moving forward with hesitant baby steps; now we watched him go by leaps and bounds.

We now augmented the SCD diet and methyl B12 injections with a vast array of supplements. Dr. Neurbrander had designed a program of vitamins, minerals, and essential oils (with fatty acids) such as cod liver oil, borage oil, and evening primrose oil. There were also probiotics, anti-yeast supplements (garlic and grapefruit seed extract), and an amino acid supplement. He put Anthony on the amino acid supplement following one of his lab tests which indicated that these essential acids were low. It was a powder compounded specifically for Anthony. This was one more factor in Anthony's progress.

In our grandparents' generation cod liver oil was the prime example of something kids hated to take. It's just one of many oils, powders and other supplements that just plain taste bad. Kids can't stand them. So how do we get autistic children—who need so many of these foul tasting mixtures—to actually get them down? With Anthony I have done it several different ways.

Mary Poppins said that a spoonful of sugar made the medicine go down. My preference is honey. I put a quarter of his vitamin mixture in Almond milk and add extra honey. He drinks it! I use to make his vitamins in a little medicine cup and mix them with a few tablespoons of juice. I would then put the mixture in a medicine dropper and hold Anthony down while squirting his vitamins in the back of his throat. I have heard of parents putting the vitamins in apple or pear sauce with a little extra honey and feeding it to their child by spoon. If you're persistent and inventive your child will eventually take the vitamins and supplements.

Through our battle with autism I was always noticing other children with similar problems. It was inevitable that I would become more attuned to certain looks, gestures, and interactions.

One day I had to go to the Pathmark store to get something for dinner. My usual habit was to go to the grocery store in the evening after Don got home. I'd learned not to bring Anthony. He couldn't contain himself, and often became the terror of the aisles. After several of these trips I'd started only going food shopping when I could leave him home. But that evening I only needed one thing. Austin and Daniella were at home with Grandma Fran, and Anthony seemed calm enough. I thought: "This will be quick. I'll chance it and see how he does."

I was so pleased when Anthony was close to perfect. He held my hand and walked next to me, not going nuts about anything. I pointed out the balloons, and got him one for being so good.

Outside on the sidewalk was one of those kids' car rides, the kind where you put in a quarter, and the kid can take the wheel for a couple of minutes. As we were leaving I saw a mother and her son at the ride. The boy was pretty big, about the size of an eight-year-old—too big for that kind of toddlers' ride. Still he tried to climb in. There was no way he could fit. As his mom pulled him away he grabbed her hand and pulled her toward it. He wasn't speaking. He just took her hand, and placed it on the car. I knew this move from Anthony. It's what a child does when there are no words.

When Anthony and I had started manding this quickly changed. When he wanted something he made sounds, sometimes words, or gave me a sign. He still pulled if he didn't know the sign or word, but he had increasingly complex ways to communicate his wants to me.

I watched, feeling as if I were seeing both the past, and a future that might have been ours if we hadn't found Anthony new ways to learn. I found myself moving toward them. I couldn't stop myself.

Anthony had taken an interest in the gum ball machine, so he was occupied for a few moments. I walked over to the boy and his mom.

"Hello," I said. "Is this your son?"

She looked gentle, but her eyes were tired. "Yes, this is Jimmy," she said. Jimmy was still pulling on her shirt as he tried to climb into the seat.

"Do you live in this town?" I asked.

"Yes, we do."

"I just wondered. I know that kind of pulling. My son over there at the gumball machine, he does that sometimes. But Jimmy's older. He must be in school by now."

"Yes," she said. "Jimmy goes to a private school about a half hour from here. He—He's like this because he has autism."

"So does Anthony." I answered.

"That little boy over there?" she asked.

"That's him," I told her.

"Why, that's hard to believe," she said. "You know, I saw you there in the store with him, and it made me think of when Jimmy was little. I was just thinking how lucky you are to have a typical little boy."

"No," I told her. "You know how it is with autism. Anthony's not typical but I have tried a lot of therapies that have helped Anthony tremendously. We follow the Defeat Autism Now protocol. It's a whole group of biomedical interventions. They've helped tremendously. Maybe they could help Jimmy. If you give me your email I'll send you some information. It can point you in the right direction."

As Jimmy kept tugging at her, and trying to climb into the impossibly small space, she said: "I know we should be better at his diet but it's so hard."

Jimmy ran around her to their cart, and went after a bottle of soda. She grabbed it and held it up. He was jumping and trying to get it, but he didn't make a sound.

"Okay," she said to him. "One more sip."

Watching this my mind flipped from biomedical to VB. The soda was all wrong, but you work with what you've got. This was a manding opportunity.

"Can I try something with him?" I asked her.

"Sure go ahead."

I took the soda bottle from her, as he turned to look at me. I had what he wanted. Our eyes met. I felt a chill run up my spine. With his big brown eyes, big cheeks and dark hair he could have easily been Anthony a few years down the road. I wanted to grab him and hug him tight. Jimmy grabbed for the soda bottle.

I held it away from him. "Soda," I said, then I paused for two seconds. "Soda," I repeated. Again I paused.

Jimmy looked at the bottle then at me. "Soooa," he said. I immediately handed him the bottle. I grinned at him. "Great job, Jimmy."

His mom looked at me. "Wow, he tried to say it."

"Sure, he did. That's called 'manding.' Really, it's just a method for getting him to ask for what he wants. Once you learn how to do it, you can get him to mand all the time, and that will be a big step in getting him to communicate."

"I know that's what he needs to do," she told me. "That's what they're supposed to be teaching him at school, but I get the feeling his teachers are just babysitting him. He does trials there, but they keep telling me he's learning what he can, and this is what we have to expect."

"Do you do anything at home?" I asked.

"We did have a home therapist who got him to cooperate during therapy. The home therapist was doing better than his teachers at school, so I taped what she was doing and sent the tape to his school. They said he was being prompted from off camera."

"Are you serious?" I asked.

"I think they've got it in their heads that Jimmy can only do a certain amount, and nothing's going to make them think otherwise," she said.

"That's crazy," I told her. "What are they teaching him at school?"

"The regular things: academic subjects... but he can't do it."

"Of course he can't. They're not letting him. How can you teach a child academic subjects when he doesn't know how to ask for a drink of water?" I said.

"I know." She shook her head.

Jimmy stood over by Anthony. They were both intent on those gumballs.

"Can I give him one?" I asked her.

"Sure," she replied.

I walked over to them and took out some quarters. "Ball," I said while I made the sign for ball. He looked at me. I grabbed his hands and prompted the ball sign. I quickly put the quarter in the machine and got a gumball, giving Jimmy a tiny piece of it. He grabbed for more. I modeled the sign for ball again and said ball. He approximated the sign. "Good, Jimmy." I gave him another piece. We did this several times. He picked it up quickly.

His mother was amazed.

"He's smart," I told his mom. "He's capable. He just needs people to work with him on that kind of stuff. He needs Verbal Behavior therapy, not only trials. He could pick it up in no time. It would mean a lot of work for you, but you'd see results, and soon everything would be easier."

"Yes. That's really something," she said.

I offered to help her, and eventually we did get in contact, and I gave her information about DAN and VB.

Jimmy haunted me. I couldn't sleep. I would wake up and think of him. Sometimes I still see him around town, and I wish I could do more.

Early Intervention is important not just for the child, but for the parents and family too. As years pass, and a child remains in the arrested stage of autism's grip, people grow used to it. They think of the condition as a given, and become convinced that change is impossible. There is still hope for children like Jimmy. Even older kids can catch on to a lot with VB, and their lives can be improved through biomedical interventions. What they need are people around them who are willing to work hard for awhile so that the child, and the family can have it easier for a lifetime.

CHAPTER OBSERVATIONS

Amino acids are essential for our bodies. They are important for detoxification, producing enzymes, hormones, antibodies, and immunoglobulins. The body needs to have proper digestion of foods in order to get adequate amino acids. Some of these come through a properly balanced diet, but some are produced inside the body. If the body is not absorbing and digesting food, this can reduce amino acid production.

Digestion problems are endemic among autistic children. This causes amino acid deficiencies which affect the ability to detoxify the body. This keeps a body from absorbing or producing the necessary amino acids. In their book "Autism: Effective Biomedical Treatments" Dr. Jon Pangborn and Dr. Sidney MacDonald Baker warn that the gut should be cleaned up before beginning amino acid supplements. If the gut is not healed the amino acids can have an adverse effect on the gut. The book suggests having a proper amino acid analysis to detect the child's deficiencies, then working closely with a doctor to put together a proper program of supplements. It will be different with every child.

Each supplement supplies different needs. For instance, there is a vital need for fatty acids. Fatty acids are the building blocks of cell walls (membranes). It is crucial to have a healthy cell wall so the material inside the cell is protected from toxins and organisms outside of the cell.

Picture the cell being a balloon filled with water. The water is the material in the cell and the balloon is the cell wall. The cell wall is made from fatty acids that are absorbed from the diet. In an autistic child's system we have to pay special attention to the types of fatty acids, because the cell wall is a sensitive point in the transmission of information throughout an organism. Omega 3 and Omega 6 oils contain many essential fatty acids. They can be found in cod liver oil, fish oil, borage oil, evening primrose oil, and flax seed oil.

Fatty acids are also essential to nerve transmission, the growth and healing processes of cells, swelling and inflammation, muscle reflexes, transporting oxygen from cells to tissues, supporting the immune system, and providing energy to the heart muscle.

Vitamin and mineral supplements are always important. Even if you feed your child the healthiest diet available today, you must take into account the toxic substances that pollute our environment. Much of our soil has been depleted of the minerals it had years ago. Even if our food is absorbing nutrients correctly, just how many nutrients are in our food? We can all benefit from multi-vitamin and mineral supplements.

CHAPTER FIFTEEN

Through all of this I had never completely ended our relationship with traditional pediatricians. Despite our disagreements about approaches to autism, I knew that in the area of traditional medicine they were competent and thorough. There were also all the usual health coverage concerns. In many cases our insurance would only cover traditional treatments. Usually I relied on them purely for annual checkups, but I also took the kids in for visits if the problem seemed to be one that needed a professional eye, and perhaps a prescription. Had anything been more serious I would have made whatever judgments were necessary, and I wouldn't have balked for an instant if I'd thought I needed a second opinion.

When I was at their offices I never hesitated to bring up details of methods and treatments I'd learned in my fight against Anthony's autism. I'm not one who believes that parents should keep their mouths shut on matters of health. I gave those doctors information on everything from heavy metal poisoning to the gut/brain connection to Verbal Behavior. Our own pediatrician would listen but seldom said too much. She seemed unaware of most of it.

One morning I had to take Daniella in to have her throat looked at. It was at a place where I'd taken all three kids for years. This was where I'd brought Anthony for many of those early problems: ear infections, bowel problems and so on. They had all the kids' records.

The practice was comprised of several women physicians, and one morning one of the other doctors confided that her son had autism. As soon as she said so I started into my spiel about things we'd tried, and things that had worked. I focused on the SCD diet, because it's always best to start with what we're putting into our kids' bodies.

"I've heard of it," she said, "but I'm not sure how I could get him to stay on it. There are so many temptations, and he just loves to eat so much."

"How are his bowels?" I asked.

"Not good," she admitted. "He has diarrhea up to seven times a day."

"Then you really should do it. I can get you information, and there are all kinds of websites with more."

"I know, but I really don't see how it could do much good. It's going to be next to impossible to keep him on it all the time."

"You should at least try it," I said. "You know, you might see results in just a few days—certainly you would begin to see changes in a couple of weeks. Don't you think you could keep him on it that long?"

"I could, but you know, there are so many things we already have to do every day.
There's his therapy, and medicines... and it seems like everyone we meet has a solution."

"I know," I said, "but this is just one thing: what he eats. I'll admit, it's a very big thing, but if you do it for a couple of weeks you just might find that it's becoming a really good habit. Then it won't be anywhere near as hard."

"I suppose so."

I could tell she wasn't exactly sold on it, but at that moment I had to take Daniella back to the examination room where we waited for our pediatrician. I felt frustrated.

One of the older pediatricians came in with Anthony's chart. As she looked it over she said: "I heard you talking about that SCD diet. Is that what you're doing with him?"

"It sure is," I replied. "He's been on it for months now. I had him on the gluten-free-casein-free diet, but that hadn't really done the job. When I heard about SCD there was a lot that seemed to make sense. I tried it, it worked, and his stools are so much better. My husband and I call them: 'champion stools.'"

She looked up at me, raising an eyebrow. "Exactly what do you feed him?"

"Nothing strange," I said. "It's based on feeding a child natural foods. He still gets carbohydrates, but it's simple ones with sugars that his gut can break down easily."

She sat down. "What else?" Though her eyes went to the chart I had the feeling she simply had to look away from me. I got the feeling that she'd taken on the role of an interrogator trying to get a suspect to talk. Well, I didn't mind talking.

"It's got everything a child needs: meats, vegetables... all the normal stuff. But it keeps out all kinds of junk food, and complex carbohydrates... foods with toxins and the kinds of sugars that are hard to break down."

"And you think this helps him?"

"Of course it does. And it's not just the diet. That's really important, but so are the methyl B12 shots, the chelation... it's a whole program."

"And you think those help him too?"

"I don't think it," I said, "I know it. Look at his chart. You have his chart here."

"Yes," she said, flipping a couple of pages on the clipboard. "It's here with your other children."

"Then it should have all this," I said. "Look where he was at eight months, twelve months, fifteen months. Then see how much better things are now. Back then we were filling him with steroids, antibiotics—"

She eyed the chart, which was full of notations about prednisone, laxatives and other prescriptions. She looked up at me. "And you think all these were mistakes?"

"I think a lot of it was. And if he needed any of it, then right afterward I should've started undoing the damage. Look at how he reacted to all that. It's right there in the record. Up to seven months he was developing normally. Then he got infections and breathing problems, and we started with all those prescriptions. When he was taking all those things he was going downhill—or he'd hit bottom. Since we started with the biomedical interventions he's been going uphill again, catching up with other kids."

She smiled. "Children have their ups and downs. There are growth spurts, and times when it seems like everything is dormant."

"There's a difference between being dormant and falling away into a fog. He didn't even know the world was there for months. He didn't know who I was. Now he's back with us again."

"And you don't think any of that was just him growing out of those problems?"

"I think he had an injured body and an injured brain and he had to heal," I said. "I think that at least some of it came because his body couldn't take the things we were putting into it, including steroids, antibiotics, and possibly some of the things in all those vaccines. And I think that's true of a lot of autistic children—maybe all of them. If we would work to heal those wounded areas then they could make incredible progress. None of you thought he was going to grow out of those things. That's not the prognosis I got—not once he'd been diagnosed with autism. At that point the pediatricians here seemed to think his prospects were pretty limited. But look what he's done."

She shrugged. "We're not always right, and I think in Anthony's case we underestimated his ability to grow out of problems. I don't think it has much to do with diet, or vitamin B-12, or any of those other things you give him. Some of those 'alternative' approaches may actually hurt him."

"But how can you say that?" I demanded. "The improvement only came when we started giving him those things."

"Coincidence," she said. "I think that as his mother you should understand that. A lot of dietary approaches have the potential to be harmful. Many diets don't include essential things. Is he getting the right proteins? Vitamins? Minerals? A growing child needs basics."

"And he gets those basics. You were asking me about SCD, not the other way around. You don't know what it includes or doesn't include. I can give you some information, and there's a lot on the web."

"There are so many diets on the web," she said. "Millions of them, and many of them aren't good diets. I think you should consider all the things Anthony's gotten besides those diets and shots of yours." Again she glanced at his chart. "He's gotten early intervention, with therapy and special education. Those things can really help some children with autism."

"And they have," I said, "once we got his therapists to try Verbal Behavior."

"So you've interfered there too," she said.

"I've gotten his therapists to try a method that works," I replied. "Don't you understand? It all works together, the diet, the supplements, the shots, and the therapy. That's why Anthony's doing so much better."

She shook her head. "I think you're living in a dream world."

"If I am, then that dream includes all those things I've just told you about," I said. "It doesn't include tubes in his ears, steroids, asthma meds, laxative prescriptions, or endless nights with no sleep. What it does include is all that's happened to Anthony while he was getting those diets and treatments and interventions. That means it includes a little boy who's making leaps and bounds, whose eyes are clear and knowing, who's now a part of his world, playing with his brother and sister, petting the dogs, and making mischief, just like any little boy. It includes that boy talking, communicating, and seeking out hugs. That's the dream world. It's one that didn't fit any of the prognoses I got early last year."

"But the relationships you're claiming can't be proved," she said. "There's nothing that shows with any certainty that any of the things you're talking about brought about his progress."

"That's what you say, but I believe in visible cause-and-effect. He was the way he was, and traditional medicine said he would stay that way. There might be limited progress, but nothing more. I refused to be or let my son be limited by that. I tried certain methods. Some of them didn't work. Others produced the exact results that they claimed they would. A few produced more than they said they would. Those methods are causes. The result is my son being able to hug back when I hug him. The result is a little boy who's starting to talk, and make sense"

"I think you're talking about a little boy who's done a very good job of growing out of some problems."

"Come on," I said. "That would take more time than he's had. I have two older children. I know how long it takes a child to 'grow out' of a physical condition. Many of these changes were almost immediate. When he went off dairy products it was almost like he stood up at attention. When he started SCD his bowel improved within a couple of weeks. The VB therapy had effects within a few days."

"You haven't proved anything," she said. "You've just told me about a whole lot of events that might occur in the normal course of growing up. Also there's the matter of perception. You want those things to work, so you think they do."

"When you treat a child, or when you write a prescription, do you want it to work?" I asked.

"Of course, but I know what I'm seeing."

"So do I," I said.

"You're wrong," she said flatly. "None of what you've described could produce the results you claim. There's no proof whatsoever."

I stared at her. "I'm sitting here, knowing what's happening to my son every day, and I'm supposed to believe that?"

"If you could be at all objective you would see my point."

"I see what's happened to Anthony," I said. "You talk about proof, but you haven't offered any. All you can say is he 'grew out of it.' He 'grew out of' poor bowel movements in two weeks. He 'grew out of' total inattention to the world in a few days. 'He grew out of it.' That's all the proof you offer. Yet preceding each improvement in each of those cases, I'd started using a method that was supposed to produce that improvement—this after a year of your medications which had him sinking deeper into autism every day. And now you tell me he just grew out of it. It's that kind of thinking that would have had me do nothing, and my son would still be sitting on the floor with vacant eyes and a slack jaw. Instead he's wide awake, and learning, because I did something about it. You should admit to the truth of the evidence right there in those records. In this other approach the doctors I've worked with are credible, and they've proved that Anthony's autism is treatable."

"You're very lucky," she said, a harsh tone creeping into her voice, "and advising others to do what you've done could be a huge mistake."

"Is my son's recovery a mistake?" I asked her. I stared at her, my voice rising.

We were both red in the face. She stood, and backed up to the door. "Let's not have this discussion because we obviously don't agree," she said.

"Isn't that all the more reason to talk it out?" I asked, trying to put a lid on my emotions.

"I have to go," she said. She opened the door and fled.

Maybe she was right to leave when she did. There are times when all common ground has fallen away. Both of us had been near the point of anger. Still, as the door closed behind her I found myself speechless. I felt as if she hadn't given me a single real answer.

A few days later I sent some literature to the doctor I'd been debating. I included a letter, trying to explain my position better:

Dear Doctor,

Last week when I was in with my daughter, Daniella Burnett, you and I had a discussion about my son, Anthony. We had some disagreements about autism and the biomedical treatments for it. Though our opinions were very different on this topic, I feel it should be discussed because that is how we learn. I believe in collaboration, especially when it comes to this epidemic. The last two years I have been dedicated to researching everything I can get my hands on. I am on the Internet for hours daily. My motivation as a mother is very different from yours. I look at both sides of every treatment. I don't' treat my son with a biomedical therapy unless I have researched it myself.

The DAN doctors are dedicated physicians. They spend countless hours with each and every parent. I do hours of work for every appointment because they encourage me to document all side effects both negative and positive. They do several lab tests to ensure my son's safety. They too, believe that it is environmental factors that contribute to the rise in autism. That is why they work so hard for this cause.

I find many physicians make judgments on DAN's protocols without first educating themselves in DAN's research. You said to me that Anthony's educational therapy may have improved him. I totally agree. His Verbal Behavior program taught him to achieve academic skills, such as requesting, labeling, receptive skills, matching, etc... However, his teachers, therapists, and the professionals in his autism program all agree that Anthony is different now in ways that can't be attributed to these methods alone. They have watched children gain skills from educational therapies, and they know the change in Anthony goes beyond that. He is becoming less literal and more typical with his social skills. He makes natural expressions and eye contact. He is more "available to learn." He is not in space anymore. His sensory issues are gone!

However, if he gets a morsel of food that is not on his diet or he misses specific supplements, he is gone again! Sometimes he is gone for a whole week. The sparkle in his eyes is absent and he becomes deaf to his name. His aggression and non-compliance escalates. He becomes a sensory mess! Until you have lived this and seen it for yourself then I can understand you being skeptical. I beg you to read through these manuals. The reference area lists the studies.

These are a gift to you. Please forward them to [the doctor with the autistic son] when you are finished. I'm happy to share info if it means that you may be more open. There are several local children being recovered through these therapies. I have talked with the parents and seen the differences. These are differences that academics don't change.

I saw my son, Anthony's health miraculously improve as soon as I took this approach in April, 2003. Now we have weaned him from Flovent, Albuterol, Pulmicort, Oraprod, antibiotics, and Lactulose! Prior to that he'd had tubes in his ears. Even after those were gone we visited the ENT for several infections. He was at the pulmonologist's office for bizarre asthma attacks. He couldn't have a bowel movement without a laxative or an enema. He couldn't catch a cold without getting awful infections in his ears and lungs. After we took the biomedical route this all stopped. I haven't needed a specialist in two years. His only medical setback came when he got a hold of food not on his diet.

When this approach fails it is almost always because it hasn't been followed 100% of the time. 100% is required in the diet or you won't see the changes. Anything less is like saying "Well, I'll quit cocaine but maybe a small hit every night won't hurt."

I don't agree with you that Anthony outgrew his illnesses. Growth is slow, while this was sudden. I hope you will look at the information I sent you. There is plenty more if you're interested. Just let me know.

Please, be open for the sake of the other children!

> Sincerely,
> Christie Burnett

***

I continued to send information to the pediatrician with the autistic child. I tried to be encouraging and supportive, and not sound like a quack. I bumped into her one night at lecture about autism. She said she was considering the diet. I tried not to be overbearing in my enthusiasm, and quietly crossed my fingers.

Not long after that I took Daniella in for her annual checkup. While I was there the pediatrician with the autistic boy stopped me. "I have to thank you," she said. "I finally tried the diet with my son. It's amazing. He's made his biggest improvements yet with it. I wanted to thank you because I wouldn't have done it if it wasn't for you."

My tears started as soon as she said it. I knew what she had been through, just as many readers must know it: from firsthand experience. I knew the heartache and the sleepless nights. But now I also knew the elation that she'd felt as she'd seen her son's eyes open again. "You made my day!" I told her, and then I started telling her about Verbal Behavior.

CHAPTER SIXTEEN

As Anthony's progress increased I finally started to see light at the end of this tunnel. I held myself back from hoping for too much, keeping as close a guard as I could on my expectations.

Balancing hopes against realism is never easy. It creates that strange feeling where you want so much to jump for joy, yet you're never quite happy enough. This coincides with the realization that there's something more you can do: the next step.

That next step seems doubly important because without it you feel as if you might start slipping back down. With autism and Anthony I also knew that there was always the chance of regressions. I'd seen them firsthand in those moments when he'd gone off his diet.

By the summer of 2004, when Anthony was more than two-and-a-half, he was saying two-to-three-word phrases. Things like "We did it" and "All wet" were becoming regular parts of his vocabulary. He could greet us each by name, and comment about the family pets.

I know I always seemed to be racing, and trying to move everything faster. Sometimes friends and family would say: "Slow down, Chris. You don't have to do everything at once. Some of it can wait till tomorrow."

Sometimes they had a point, especially if I was allowing myself to get too frazzled. That kind of thing can lead to a breakdown. At the same time I'm a naturally energetic person. Also, there's the nature of the problem itself: with autism you can't let up. The child has to stick to the diet, and, if you can clearly see what the next move is in therapy or treatment, it's best to make it now. If he's mastered one thing, it's time to master the next.

So I would say to everyone: "You have to understand: he's come here from a place where everything was dark. I sat with him through those nights, and watched him stare at nothing all day. I knew a little boy whose whole world was inside a brain that couldn't experience the world, and might never have the chance to again. Now he's coming back to us one step at a time—but it's as if a clock is ticking. Every day it feels as if time might run out. I never know if this step forward is the last one. We have momentum, but it's a fragile momentum. We have to keep it going. I know that because I've seen what happens when the autism monster gets the jump on you. That's when I lose my son. That monster's not gone—not yet. I've managed to get my fingers on Anthony's hand, but autism still has his other hand. It wants to pull him down into the water and drown him. I've got to pull him up here into the boat with the rest of us. The boat is rocking; our fingers are slippery. I'm just getting my grip, and he's just gulped in his first breath, but he's a long way from being out of the water."

In July, 2004 I wrote in my diary: "Anthony had another leap in skills. Last weekend he really started understanding language. I said to him: 'Give this to Daniella,' and he did. I said: 'Throw the banana peel in the garbage.' He picked it up, walked into the kitchen and threw it away! Anthony spilled some water on the floor so I told him to get a towel and clean up the floor. He did it!"

He understood so much of what we were saying to him. With this, and his phrasemaking, he was becoming a pretty good little communicator.

***

By the end of the summer we were nearing a time when we would have to make decisions, and find new alternatives for Anthony. There was a certain bittersweet feeling in seeing him age out of his Early Intervention routines. I could certainly see successes. The team that had come together to help Anthony had done well. He could do things that many people had never dreamed he would do. But it was also time to find new ways of learning.

The basic components would remain the same: diet, biomedical methods, and Verbal Behavior. But I needed to find a school where these approaches would be respected and implemented. I've noted one of the first stops I made in my search for a school that truly used a VB approach. That was the one with the food on the floor, and the distracted staff, that I'd seen on the same day I had my breakdown the previous March. I'd come away from that all the stronger in my conviction that we couldn't allow all of our work to fall victim to that sort of thing.

So for six months I searched for a school where the implementation of Verbal Behavior lived up to the promise of the ideas. This search wasn't easy. Often I would hear: "Oh, yes, we use some of the methods of Verbal Behavior. We like to be eclectic." As I would investigate further that kind of talk became a red flag to me. Mixing VB with other approaches often achieves nothing but an undisciplined sloppiness. In such cases terms like "eclectic," "different," and "in the mix" may turn out to be nothing more than excuses for a lack of any kind of consistency. They have often fooled themselves into thinking that their attempts to use all of these different methodologies are aimed at giving each individual student what he or she needs. Instead they wind up with nothing but a hodgepodge based on whatever method might put a damper on that day's disaster. The goal becomes that of a relatively peaceful classroom, rather than a bright-eyed, learning child. Beware of such programs. Most turn out to be nothing like Verbal Behavior. How can a program work if you don't really follow it? It is programs like those which saddle VB with a reputation as a "flavor of the month." Don't let them fool you.

That is what I learned as I visited school after school. I saw kids sitting at tables, being drilled for over an hour in the old, tired way. I saw programs billed as "VB" where there was no behaviorist, no pairing, no manding, and teachers who had little or no idea of what these things were. I saw programs where no records were kept, so progress was always a vague guess made by an overloaded teacher. Where was the Verbal Behavior? Some thought "pointing programs" were VB. Other "VB" programs didn't believe in sign language for the non-vocal child. In the few schools that did use sign language the children started on difficult concepts that often didn't apply to the here-and-now issues of a child's needs and desires.

When you look for a good VB program watch out for ones that start signing with "more," "break," or "help." These are advanced signs. Watch out for ones that spend a lot of time on pointing at things right in front of them, when they should be teaching children to ask for things that aren't out in plain sight. Look for programs where children pair with the teachers in class before the teachers begin placing demands on the kids. Try to familiarize yourself with some of the terminology of Skinner's Verbal Operants. You don't have to know the whole system, but be clear about manding, pairing and a few other vital terms. If the teachers can't talk the lingo, that's a bad sign.

I was adamant in my search, and that, mixed with some luck, helped me finally find what Anthony needed: a preschool where they employed the real thing: Verbal Behavior. I met the director, and found she was truly knowledgeable. This woman wasn't just throwing terminology around. She'd been trained in places I'd heard of, and when I quizzed her she spoke with the knowledge and understanding of a professional. She said it was routine to always pair the children with teachers, aids, and other children first thing. She understood manding. The kids I saw weren't sitting, doing drills. I saw a place that could help Anthony make more progress. I saw the beginnings of his formal, outside-the-home education.

Still, no transition is without its little heartbreaks. It was a chapter in our lives closing. Anthony's therapists had been there in our home for many hours, week-in-week-out. They'd stuck with us as we'd watched him blossom. They'd endured his regressions. They'd learned Verbal Behavior methods with me, and helped to create a VB program even though none of us had formal training in it. They'd had the courage to be a part of an adventure, and they were due much of the credit for making the whole thing work. How could our parting be anything but difficult?

I decided to take a picture of each of them with Anthony. I framed each photo and on top I put a copy of a poem I found: "Everyday Heroes." That's exactly what Anthony's therapists were: a team of everyday heroes.

Here was a working team of therapists trained in Skinner's analysis of Verbal Behavior. They had seen it succeed with Anthony, fulfilling its promise. From that experience they had come to truly believe in it. Yet they worked for an agency that didn't just ignore VB; it opposed it.

This became clear to me in the following weeks and months. With Anthony in school I had some time on my hands, and at first I was beginning to wonder what to do with it.

Then one afternoon I got a call from a mother who had been referred to me by a therapist. The mother was scared to the point of being shaken to the core. Her son had just been diagnosed with autism. There she was, exactly where I had been, at the start of the struggle. She'd begun looking into it, and had heard of VB. The therapist who referred her to me had told her about the creation of Anthony's VB program.

"Yes, we did that," I said.

"But how did you do it? The agency is so against it," she said. "When I asked them they said VB is only for older children."

"I know they have people who are against it in younger children" I said, "but to me that didn't make sense. It seems to me that you want to start out by teaching a child how to ask for the things he or she desperately wants. That's how a child learns to want to communicate."

"That's what I've heard, and it makes sense to me too, but they have a speech pathologist who doesn't believe in it, so now they're all against it, at least the ones in their office."

"Wow," I said. "I knew there was a lot of misinformation about it, but I didn't know it was that bad. But it's not impossible. I put a team together for Anthony, and it really worked."

"That's what I was told," she said, "but I wouldn't know where to start."

"I'll be glad to send you some information about free workshops," I said. "They have them periodically in the area. I'll also send along some stuff you can read about how it all works. You can start by focusing on pairing and manding with your son every day, throughout the day. Mand with him as much as possible. Even that much will help. But then you need to talk to your son's team about trying it. You might have to persuade them. That's what I did."

We talked for an hour. When I hung up the phone I called Laura.

"You know, this isn't the first time," I said.

"I know," Laura said. "You've told me. You've heard from a lot of parents like her, haven't you?"

"A lot," I agreed.

"It's so sad, Christie. These poor kids have no chance," Laura said, "and the EI agency doesn't seem to get it at all."

"I'm going to call them," I said. "If I offer to do the legwork necessary to get their therapists trained, maybe they'll do it. I could do a fundraiser to get the money for it, and Alexis could do the actual training."

"Go for it Christie, I'll help you." Laura replied.

I started putting in calls to the director of our Early Intervention Provider agency that afternoon. I left several messages. She didn't bother to reply, so I decided to write her a letter. In the letter I described the problem, proposed my solution asked for a meeting between agency representatives, parents and therapists. I was polite, positive, and I emphasized working together. I never went beyond asking for a discussion of possibilities.

This drew a phone call from the director. She stated the agency's opposition to using Verbal Behavior techniques, and gave the reasons for that opposition.

"You have to understand," she said, "that the New Jersey Health Department opposes Verbal Behavior."

"That's official?" I asked.

"I suppose that depends on what you mean by official."

"That it's in a law or a guideline," I said.

"I'm not sure if it's currently in any guideline, but if I had to I'm sure I could get a Health Department official to put that opposition in writing. They don't want it, and, as you know, they give us funding. In addition to that, one of our best speech therapists, a woman whose opinion is well-respected, thinks poorly of Verbal Behavior."

"People said a lot of things about B.F. Skinner and Behaviorism decades ago. But this is a method that's working today."

"You believe that, but you are not a professional."

"No," I said. "My only official qualification is that I'm a mom. And my son's only official qualification is that he's a little boy with autism, and he's recovering."

She sighed. "Ms. Burnett, I'm glad your little boy is recovering. I really am, and I mean that from the bottom of my heart. But I simply can't believe the Verbal Behavior is responsible for what you are seeing. Verbal Behavior is popular this week, but next week it'll be swimming with dolphins, or placing magnets around a child's skull. I've seen these things come and go, Ms. Burnett. All of them have a few success stories, but unfortunately we can't change policy just to fit a few cases. If we did we'd have all the children putting on magnetic skullcaps one week, and swimming with dolphins the next. I'm not blaming you or criticizing you. I'm sure you've done wonders with your son. But sometimes when we really believe in something it seems to work."

"Anthony didn't believe in anything," I said. "He didn't even believe in me. He couldn't. When we started he couldn't perceive enough to care. Now he can, and does, and Verbal Behavior has a lot to do with it. I saw it work with him, and with others too. When you see it work, you see why it works, and how much it goes with simple common sense. Isn't that a good basis for policy?"

"You speak as a true believer," she said, but that was as far as she would go.

We went on for a few minutes, but it was the same conversation I'd had with our pediatrician some weeks before. Though this was about education, and that had been about diet and medicine, the attitudes were the same. At one point the director said outright that VB was nothing but a fad. By that time I wasn't going to bother to point out that this "fad" had been producing successful results for decades. I'd resigned myself to the knowledge that I was at a dead end with her. Instead I asked what I was supposed to tell parents who wanted this "fad." She suggested I tell them to go to another agency.

"There are no other agencies around here that do VB," I said.

"I suppose that's true, and I've just told you all the reasons for that," she said.

I was up against a painfully familiar brick wall. I understood that much of her opposition was rooted in bureaucratic inertia. You have people trained in one method, and that is a large investment of money and time. No doubt the current method works a little better than what preceded it. That creates a reason to keep it. She'd spoken of belief, but that can work two ways. When you've gone through the process of learning a system, it's always going to be easier to keep believing in it. The EI agency had its system, and they weren't going to change easily.

She'd noted that I wasn't a professional in the field. That was true. I wasn't a bureaucrat either. I was simply a mother who had looked at every alternative I could find, then tried something different and seen it work much better than the conventional approach. I had a son who was well on his way to full recovery, and I had seen successes with other children as well. My son and I had barely survived with the stunted expectations and grim failures of the old school. I knew its limitations, and I knew what could be achieved outside it.

Verbal Behavior isn't an easy path. Retraining a therapist takes time and money. In some ways it's harder to grasp, especially when you've been trained in other techniques. It's not a simple recipe. But it works. I knew this from experience, and no amount of bureaucratic inertia could change that knowledge. I was at a point where I had to do something.

It was time.

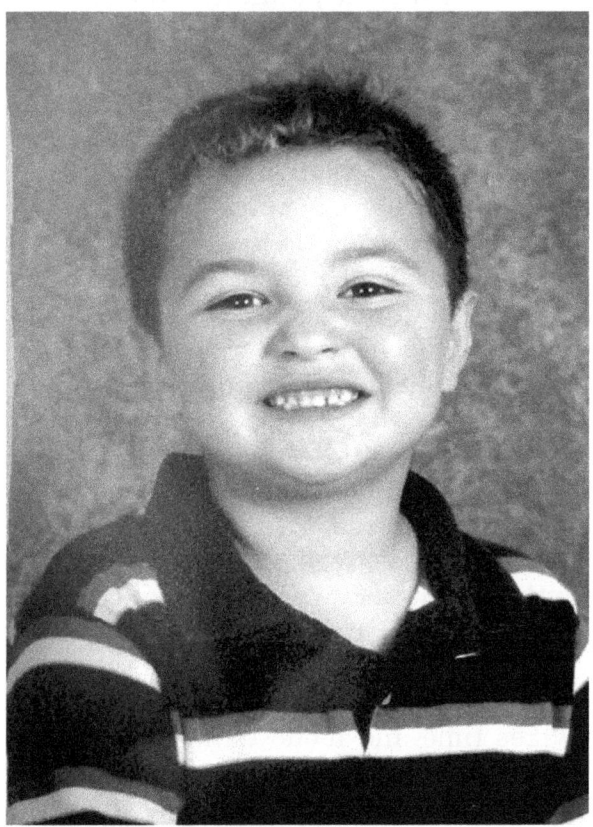

CHAPTER SEVENTEEN

By this time I could see how the pieces fit together: the body and the mind. When you treat a child's physical problems it opens the pathways to the brain. The child can finally see and hear the world, and is open to a wide range of experiences that would have been impossible before.

I'd found many allies in the battle, from those I'd met in health food stores, to holistic physicians, to people in pediatrics, and finally Anthony's therapists. True, the traditional medical establishment wasn't enthusiastic about biomedical approaches, and the educational system's response had been severely limited, but if you looked you could find the ones who could help.

The biggest problem was putting it all together into a single approach. I had begun doing it without even realizing that this was the aim. I had been lucky in the methods I'd stumbled upon and the people I'd found. Gradually it had all come together. But now I saw there was a need to help other parents do this with their autistic children. From my own experience I knew just how much work it took just to find information. Even if you worked hard, it was clear that there was luck involved. What if I had lived in a place where there had been no conferences or meetings within hundreds of miles? What if I'd never found Dr. Neubrander and Alexis, and all the others who had helped? What if I hadn't had the advantages I'd had from the start?

Also, while I'd discovered all these pieces of a successful way to attack autism, I hadn't seen them synthesized into a unified approach. There had to be a way to systematize this so parents wouldn't be so dependent on luck. I needed to create a way to put all the components together in a lot of cases instead of just one.

Parents needed to learn how to clean out their children's bodies, then there had to be a way to train therapists, form teams, and link them with the children who were ready. When children were ready there was a need to get them into well-designed educational programs in the school system.

I decided to try to make that happen in my part of New Jersey. I would start a company that would act as a point of contact for parents, teachers, therapists and school systems. I wanted to show other parents, teachers and therapists how to do what we had done for Anthony I also wanted to start a Moms Night Out group that could get parents together in our area to help trade information we had learned and mentor new parents just starting this journey. I would work with the parents myself, showing them where to find the resources for the SCD diet. I would take them from store to store if I had to. Laura wanted to help me. We would show them how to read labels, a create substitutions, creating diets that would make a child ready and willing to learn.

Laura and I started talking to our teams of therapists. After all we'd learned together there was no reason for these women to drift back into traditional trialing methods. Between us we had seven people trained in VB.

With the resources I had discovered I began Aspiring Angels Therapy, LLC. I spoke to a lawyer and an accountant, and I went to the bank. I registered the name, and started the process of making everything official.

I called Alexis. "If I can get a team together, can you help us train the therapists?" I asked her.

"Of course I can," she said.

The seven therapists Laura and I had were the core. We got a seven-hour lecture series about Verbal Behavior methods on a DVD, then got the local library to give us space for several free workshops. We also invited both therapists and mothers who were interested in learning more about Verbal Behavior. The reaction to our first workshop was amazing. As we showed the lecture series the therapists saw how things worked (and how their own methods didn't work) right there on the screen. They watched how the children reacted to VB methods. Many of these therapists came away ready to try them.

"I see myself up there," one therapist told me, gesturing at the screen. "It's all right there: so much of what's not working. Now I can see why the Verbal Behavior methods might work much better. I'm willing to try."

Those kinds of comments kept me going.

The parents loved it as well. On different weekends we worked with different groups. My father and Don helped with the technical equipment, so we could concentrate on the content of the workshops. Things went well because all of us really cared.

By January, 2005 we were ready to begin training in earnest. This was where Alexis took over. With her there we never had any problems keeping people interested; everyone hung on her every word. The hours flew by like minutes. In no time we had a great team of fourteen motivated therapists. I called New Jersey's Department of Health and Senior Services. We needed to go through them to be approved for Early Intervention programs covering children from one to three. Once I had contacted the department, I started the enrolling process so we could get each therapist approved. I wanted Aspiring Angels to be able to work with families, schools, counties and the state. I knew the paperwork would be daunting, but after battling against my own son's autism for two years I just assumed I could do it.

Red tape is always time consuming, and this was no exception. I had already covered the basic business legalities: EIN number, and registration. Now I needed to make sure everything was official and approved in terms of each individual therapist. The state sent me an unsigned contract explaining that all of the therapists would have to be approved before the final, signed contract came through. It would take at least six months. Welcome to the real world, Christie!

But that didn't mean we couldn't start other aspects of our mission right away. Though we were limited in what we could do in formal therapy and educational settings, we could start working with individual children right away. We did this in home programs, and soon we were able to establish ties with local school districts, providing therapists for home programs that augmented what happened in classrooms. Meanwhile I continued to recruit more therapists, and set them up with training with Alexis.

At this writing I'm still doing that. I also work closely with the parents. That, after all, is how I came into all this. I know first hand what they are going through. I try to get to know each parent and child, matching them with therapists who best fit their personalities and situations.

In the Spring of 2005, while waiting for the cogs of bureaucracy to turn, Aspiring Angels began a play group for autistic kids. Every time I'd visited social groups for these children the activities had seemed forced. An autistic child would walk in the door, and suddenly there would be an introduction: "Say hi to Ricky!" Often the other kid could care less about Ricky.

The same kinds of assumptions and expectations went into the activities themselves. An adult might sit a child down in front of a train set with the idea that the child will set the train on the track, and push it, but the child might not have the slightest idea how the train and track go together. Without that context the child won't even try. These are the kinds of things you shouldn't do until certain skills are already in place. A play area may be the place to develop them, but the skills won't happen on their own. In the social settings I'd seen there was often no allowance for kids who were just beginning to learn.

We wanted to create a play group where teachers would set up situations designed so that children could interact in ways that fit their various skill levels. In such a group teachers would help social processes along by helping children of different learning levels communicate. The playgroup sessions were based on Verbal Behavior and focused on pairing children together with reinforcement to create a bond that will be the basis of developing higher level social skills. Children who are in the early learning stage can begin by pairing one child with another. For example if Anthony loves blocks and Emily loves puzzles you can prompt Anthony to give Emily a puzzle piece. You would then quickly reinforce Anthony by giving him a favorite toy or edible such as a piece of cookie. Then you can prompt Emily to give Anthony a block. Again reinforce Emily for doing this as well. You would repeat this several times. This can begin the process of pairing. Once the children seem interested in one another you can prompt the children to request reinforcers from one another. If a bond is developed between them you can contrive more appropriate play situations. If they both love to jump put them on the trampoline together and bounce them up and down. As long as they are having fun together it is a huge step toward social skills. For more advanced learners you can teach the children to ask "wh" questions. This would be manding for information. A child might ask another child where a certain toy was, but the teacher would be there to make sure everything was ready for both the question, and the response. If Ricky loves cars, you can contrive a situation where he will look for them. Maybe have the container they are always in lying on the floor so Ricky goes up to it and looks down at it; however no cars are in it. Prior to this you've set the cars over with Sarah.

You can prompt Ricky by saying "What do you want?" If he says: "Cars," you reply: "I don't have them, but Sarah knows where they are." You help by walking over to Sarah with Ricky. Again you prompt Ricky to say: "Sarah, do you know where the cars are?" Sarah might have special needs as well. If so, make sure she receives the proper prompts to help her interact with Ricky. You constantly reinforce both children through this process. Prompts and other reinforcers will help both children begin the process of pairing.

A therapist helps children through the phases of manding and pairing with each other, just as they have learned to mand and pair with the therapist. The more the children are guided through this process, the more they will do it with each other without any prompts from the therapist. It was this kind of individual attention that was lacking in many groups I saw.

In our play group it was much simpler. We didn't have advanced learners, so we could rely on bigger activities set up around the room. We had a baby pool filled with dried beans, small balls, and dry rice. We also had a sensory tunnel, an inflatable jumping toy, a giant hollow ball the kids could climb into, an art area, bubbles and scooters. We asked the parents to bring their favorite edibles and small toys. Though I would have preferred to be sure that all the edibles were part of the SCD diet, I didn't want to turn people away. For this reason I gently encouraged SCD foods, but didn't require them. We did make sure that each child got only those foods that his or her parents brought, or foods from goodie bags that we'd prepared ourselves.

We also had typical children there. Typical children are always a help in modeling play. I gave goodie bags to the typical children, making sure each of them had his or her own buddy from among the special needs children. Each typical child would wear an apron with that special needs child's favorite reinforcers. The typical child would give reinforcers constantly while engaging the special needs child in play with a favorite toy. Once they were paired we could turn this into more appropriate play that could help them interact with each other. We would put three little ones in a big box and push them around the room. They loved it! We would jump together while delivering reinforcers.

In this way the autistic children learned to enjoy play. We asked nothing of them, and we delivered fun. We offered a wide range of things to do, and used manding, pairing and other tools to get the ball rolling. After that it was an hour filled with the autistic children getting to simply be kids. Bonds formed naturally as everyone had a good time.

***

As of this writing Aspiring Angels is still in the enrolling process with Early Intervention. Though the play groups have been on a brief hiatus while I've worked on this book, we want to resume them soon.

We've set up home programs with children, ages three-to-eight to provide VB in the home along with parent training. Sometimes we are contracted by the child's school to provide this. In other cases the family hires us privately. My dream for the agency is to start a school for children with autism using Verbal Behavior techniques. I am also laying the groundwork for more involvement as an advocate, raising awareness of VB as a teaching method with state and local agencies.

CHAPTER EIGHTEEN

In March of 2005 I had another evaluation set up for Anthony with the neurodevelopmental pediatrician. This appointment would be with a pediatrician who was new to Anthony, Dr. F. The doctor who had originally diagnosed Anthony had moved on.

As Don, Anthony and I pulled into the parking garage of the hospital I felt my nerves tighten. I remembered the smell of this garage, and the associations weren't good. The smell brought back memories of Anthony's original diagnosis, and all that went with it. The sound of our clanking footsteps in the metal stairwell just sharpened those memories. I saw the same graffiti on the stairwell walls. This was where our battle with autism had officially started. It was the place where the monster had been given its name. I wondered how many parents had come here and had their hearts broken, and how many children had left here, sentenced to a life behind a silent stare.

Now I was bracing myself. I knew I was on the home turf of the medical establishment, and anything I said about Anthony's diet, treatment or therapies was likely to be challenged. As we got to the floor where the offices were I glanced at Don, glad he was there. With his support I wouldn't have to rely so much on my own strength. As we entered the waiting room, and let them know we were there, I put on my poker face.

Dr. F came out to greet us. She sat down across from us and began asking questions. I was certain that it was inevitable for all the controversy to surface. I didn't hold back about Verbal Behavior. I mentioned one workshop, and she said: "Yes, I've been to workshops on VB myself."

I looked at her, surprised. "What did you think?" I asked.

"It's an effective approach," she said. "I've recommended it to several parents."

As we continued to talk I realized she had really looked into this, so I told her about what we had done with Anthony, and I went into detail about the fine results.

"I've even started a company," I said. "Aspiring Angels. We're working on getting accreditation for our therapists, and we're already linking parents, schools and therapists so that they can work together."

"That's good to know," she said. "I'm curious to hear more, but first let's look at Anthony."

The examination went beautifully. Though he'd been ill with a stomach virus only days before, he had no major problems. He made the transition to the examination room smoothly, and when Dr. F did anything to engage him he paid attention. He responded appropriately to every stimulus.

"He's doing so well," she said. "I'd say Anthony has made terrific progress in a very short time."

At this point I put the match to the other fuse, saying: "Well, I'm a DAN mom. I believe the biomedical therapies we've used have played a big part in Anthony's improvements." I said.

She smiled. "That's good. I don't have anything bad to say about proper dietary interventions. With Anthony doing this well all I can say is: keep doing what you're doing. Whenever parents mention diet I tell them that they should try things that are safe and nutritious. I don't push them, but I know that diet is an important part of any health equation."

As you might imagine, I liked Dr. F. She was down to earth and easy to talk to, and she felt that Anthony's prognosis was excellent. In her report she wrote: "Anthony Burnett is a three-year-four-month old boy who on neurodevelopmental assessment, has made impressive gains, but continues to show a weakness in language and personal-social skills. He has very mild Pervasive Developmental Disorder symptoms with an excellent prognosis, as he has strong cognitive skills and has certainly developed language."

Later I looked at this, and kept reading over and over "very mild Pervasive Developmental Disorder." I knew that the "very" wasn't typical wording. "Mild" would have been standard. Adding the "very" meant that she had thought about it, and knew how great Ant's progress really was. She was saying he was much further along than anyone would have predicted—that he was truly healing. I whispered aloud: "Very mild," savoring the phrase. It may seem like a small thing, but when you are still in the midst of the struggle against autism, every small step should be celebrated. The fact that this, and all of what we'd heard, came from a pediatrician in traditional medicine made it all that much better.

***

Dr. F has remained as our neurodevelopmental pediatrician. A year later, at Anthony's second appointment with her, she was still excited about his progress.

"He's really coming along," she said. "You're continuing with the Verbal Behavior, I imagine."

"We are," I replied, "and you don't know how much I love hearing you ask it that way. It's so nice to have a pediatrician who understands the value of VB."

"Oh, I do," she said. "And now certainly wouldn't be a time to halt the progress he's making with it. Anthony still needs the VB to help him with his language."

"But he's doing well, isn't he?" I asked.

"Oh, yes. You don't have to worry about that. I was impressed with his progress when you were here the last time—especially considering the records of where he'd been a couple of years ago—and I'm even more impressed now. He has some residual traces of autism, but his social and sensory issues are gone. He is speaking in sentences and conversing with me. I'm removing the diagnosis of autism. What he has now is called 'language processing delay.' There's still work to be done, but I fully expect that by next year we'll be looking at a full recovery."

I heard those words: "removing the diagnosis of autism" and I felt light-headed. "That means so much," I said.

"I can imagine," she said, looking at Anthony. "You know, this appointment has warmed my heart."

I thanked her, and left there feeling even better than I had the year before. We had come so far, and her words confirmed it.

It took me awhile to come back to earth where there was still plenty of work left to do. Of course, we went on with VB, as well as with the biomedical and SCD parts of our program. Anthony has progressed, day-to-day, week-to-week, and every day he continues to be a miracle, just like any other little boy.

***

Anthony's recovery is nearly complete, but what really tells you your little boy is back is what you see out in the world, rather than in an examination room.

One Saturday last February the weather forecasters predicted that we were going to get a huge snowfall that night. I was looking forward to it. Sunday morning we wouldn't have work or have school to deal with, and a good, deep snow would be a great excuse to just hang around indoors, not even getting out of our pajamas if we didn't feel like it. I love snow, but the New Jersey winter had been on the warm side, and it had been awhile since we'd seen much of the white stuff.

The next morning we woke up to that crystal white world of new fallen snow. All sounds were muffled by the soft white cover on the ground, and the flakes were still falling. The weather forecasters were calling for a foot or more. That was fine by me. I stood at the window for a moment admiring it. The pine trees were frosted, and the world had that soft look that only comes with a fresh layer of snow.

A half hour later Don was outside shoveling, and I was in the kitchen making pancakes. The kids saw Don, and wanted to run right out the door.

"Not yet," I said. "Those pancakes will be ready in a minute."

The idea of pancakes and syrup just barely kept them indoors. It snowed all day. We watched movies and cuddled on the couch, letting nature do its work outside. Right after dinner the phone rang. It was our neighbors' children from across the street.

"Can Austin and Daniella come outside to play in the snow?" they asked.

We'd expected this. For years whenever it's snowed, Austin and Daniella pile on warm clothes, and join the neighbors to play in the snow, but once Anthony was old enough to be mobile we always had to camouflage the activity. We would get them out of his line of vision, dressed them, then sneak them out the back door. It had to be that way because Anthony hadn't been ready for this kind of freeform activity. If it wasn't a cold or infection, there were always the many other difficulties that came with autism.

You have to be very close to them at all times. I always felt it was like I was trapped in that early toddler state with Anthony.

But this night was different. Don and I decided it was time to let Anthony join them. Anthony was very excited. In the past he wouldn't have tolerated all the extras: the snowsuit, gloves and scarf. Now he wanted to jump into his suit. Once he got his scarf and hat on he looked like the little boy he was: adorable. The only things visible under the layers were two big cheeks and his eyes.

Don and I watched as the kids crossed the street to our neighbors' house. There were no cars, and barely a sound could be heard. The night had the stillness that only the snow can provide. The sky was clearing, and the snow shone in the light from our houses. I stood in the doorway and watched.

Anthony played. Yes, all the other kids played too, and I always loved watching Austin and Daniella having fun, but that night my eyes were on Anthony. Somewhere far back in my mind, were memories of coughs, the stark light of emergency rooms and doctor's offices, and the long hours of therapy, but those images were finally receding. Here was my son, calling out, running, falling, and helping to build a snowman. He rode on a sleigh, made snow angels, and held his own in a snowball fight. Don and I couldn't take our eyes off of him. It was as if we were dreaming.

Finally the time was past when we'd had to take turns sneaking to this door to watch Austin and Daniella play, while the other stayed behind with Anthony in front of the TV. Now all three of our kids were out there, playing together. My eyes welled up. Don rubbed my back, knowing exactly what I was thinking.

"I could stand here all night and watch him," Don said.

"So could I."

"We did it, didn't we?"

"We did."

We stood there hearing the children's playful voices, and for the first time in years we realized that all of us were free. We had worked hard, and Anthony had worked hardest of all, using the tools we'd given him to break loose of the prison in his brain. Together we had found a way for Anthony to be a child playing with all the others in the snow.

Appendices

Appendix I
Daily Routines and Regular Calendar Events

While I've focused on the life of the child, I should also tell you a little about the changes in the life of your whole household. Autism alters daily routines. It will do this whether you concentrate on the illness or not, so you might as well concentrate on the illness. Doing so will give your child and your whole family the best chance for recovery.

One thing you have to get used to with autism is the busy routine of your day-to-day life. It's not easy to adjust to all the people who pass through your home. Every day there are therapists and teachers. When they aren't there you're probably on the phone, or out getting the various supplies. If you have other children you have to incorporate all their needs in with this overarching goal of defeating autism. You, your spouse, your family, and all those who are close with you, are all affected.

A great deal of this defies description. Some tasks and habits slip into your life as the needs arise, and slip out when those needs ebb. Other things are there all the time. You adjust to them, then can't recall how life was without them.

In this section I want to outline some of the most important things that take up the days of the parents of an autistic child.

I've written about all the vitamins and supplements that Anthony needed. If I'd seen the list of all of these at the start I would have certainly panicked. My fears might have overwhelmed me completely if I'd realized that I was going to have to sort them out, and mix certain ones according to specific formulas each day. There were moments when groups of these were added to my list (for instance, on some visits to Dr. Neubrander), when I did panic. But, as with any complex set of motions, I found the shortest ways to do everything. With repetition this job became just another part of my routine. I got it down to about 10 minutes—not much more than packing your kid a good lunch before school. Also, this task is getting a little easier all the time. The manufacturers are now combining a lot of these mixtures into single pills and doses.

Once I put all these things together I had to make sure Ant took them. This could be a job in itself, but once again, it became habit. Another thing that helped was when there was a particular supplement or vitamin that had brought Ant a specific benefit. There's nothing like a good result to get you going. This certainly applied to Anthony's Methyl B-12 shot. I've written about how hard it was to give him a needle, but when the long terms results started showing themselves (which began within a few days) I got used to giving it to him.

Other treatments are easier, such as giving Ant his transdermal cream medicine, almond milk, and SCD snacks such as brownies and carrot curls. He gets many of these things more than once a day, and some of them I have to mix up, but these are tasks that have become habit.

In the evening, when it's bath time, I have to remember to put Epsom salts and lavender oil in with Ant's bath water. That's followed by his nighttime supplements such as magnesium. After I've put him to bed I wait until he's sleeping, then rub on more transdermal cream. This is for chelation.

Even then I'm not quite done. Once the kids are in bed, I usually get on the Internet to research any new treatments out there, carefully going over parents' comments about what works and what doesn't. I comment myself whenever I have something to say.

Throughout the day I'm always looking for new opportunities to target new skills, and to sharpen old ones. You never stop being a strategic scientist. You are always looking for things that work.

If all of this sounds overwhelming, I can only say: You can do it. Many other parents do. The tasks don't come all at once. You learn one thing at a time, incorporating each new skill and therapy in with the others. How do you get everything else done? You learn what's important, and what's not. You discover ways to do necessary tasks more efficiently. Also, though you're sure to stumble here and there, ultimately you will do most things as well or better than before.

And now that you know that, I can tell you about things that don't come up every day, but must be done periodically. These are more like projects that are ongoing, but only need attention now and then.

One is the chelation challenge. I plan a Sunday around this. This is how you find out what metals your child is dumping. On a day when you do this you need to collect your child's urine over a 6-hour period, then prepare the lab work. The results from this may result in changes in supplements, vitamins, dosages, and so on. You do it every 8 weeks.

I've described my preparations for appointments with Dr. Neubrander. When you have something like this, it's worth it to do the work well. Fill out the forms, answer the questions, and write a detailed summary of progress or regressions. You may have supplement sheets to fill out. While you're doing all this you'll probably find you have questions. Write them down. If you've heard about treatments that interest you, this is the time to note them.

You'll probably have these appointments almost every month at first, but as your child progresses they will go to every 2 or 3 months.

It's valuable to keep track of conferences and meetings in your area. These are the places where you can compare notes with many parents and professionals, and find out about the latest advances. The most important ones are conferences of the National Autism Association, Defeat Autism Now (DAN), and Verbal Behavior workshops. Also search out local support groups.

You'll need to schedule an appointment at your local hospital now and then for blood work. You'll want them to look at vitamin and mineral levels, and liver function. At first you'll do these every 5 weeks or so, but eventually your child should only need this monitoring 3 times a year.

Last but not least is the stool analysis. You'll be dividing your child's stool into several vials, preparing a lab kit, and mailing it into the lab. Luckily this might only happen every 6 months, though it will be more if there are severe bowel problems.

There's no question that it's a lot to do, but consider what you do for any child. Most of us take on all the duties of raising typical children without considering all of the consequences. They are born, and suddenly they fill our entire lives. An autistic child just fills your life more, and if you face the challenge, and do the work, you will see results, just as you would with any child. Life itself is overwhelming; is that any reason to turn away?

Appendix II
NAET Therapy

Of the various treatments I describe in this book, this one may be the most difficult for traditional medical practitioners to accept. Those of us who have been brought up under the care of modern medicine (especially Western medicine) tend to doubt methods that don't look traditional. But I had learned to accept a lot while battling Anthony's autism, and I was able to open my eyes to NAET.

Nambudripad's Allergy Elimination Treatment, or NAET is an alternative treatment aimed at allergies, and it has been shown to help autistic children. This holistic method was developed by Dr. Devi Nambudripad in 1983. It is used to eliminate allergies from the child.

To understand how it works, we start with the brain and central nervous system. Both of these are affected by the food we eat and the vaccines we receive, as well as chemicals, heavy metals, pollen, dust and whatever else may enter our bodies. Sometimes our reactions are negative to the point of being noticeable factors in our health. When this happens we call it an "allergic reaction." These happen when the body sees these invaders as poison, and acts to defend itself. The body may try to expel the invader. To do this it may produce something like a sneeze or a rash, or, in extreme situations, shut down certain bodily functions. These things are the allergic reactions. The aim of NAET is to get the body to accept allergens so that they can pass through the system without causing harm. NAET treatments neutralize the adverse effects so that the body can tolerate these substances.

The treatment combines elements of acupuncture, kinesiology, chiropractic, and allopathy. It is based on the idea that our bodies are made up of energy pathways called meridians. If these meridians are blocked, electrical energy stops traveling freely between the brain and nerve cells. The electrical impulses become disorganized, fragmenting, or destroying the information contained in the energy, much like a radio signal that's being jammed. This blockage results in allergic reactions, and eventually can contribute to long term illnesses, such as autism.

For centuries doctors in China have based much of their medical approach on the study and manipulation of the meridians. Now they use radioactive tracer isotopes to see the pathways more clearly. Because the meridians extend throughout the body, any problem affects the whole body, even if the symptoms only show themselves in one spot. Solutions must deal with the whole body.

When dealing with the meridians the goal is to balance the body's energy flow. NAET does this, applying itself to the entire patient, and not just one limb or organ. The therapy addresses all aspects of a patient's world: physical, physiological and emotional. NEAT clears the adverse energies of allergens, helping to detoxify the body. It clears the pathways, allowing the body to replenish its supply of vital energy.

I take Anthony to an NEAT practitioner, Mira Champaneria. Mira has dedicated herself to those who have autism. In November 2005 Mira was asked to participate in a study of children with autism who were undergoing NAET treatments. The one-year study is ongoing at this writing, with some of its participants getting treatments, while others act as controls.

Anthony has been doing NAET for several months, and we have cleared about thirty allergies. My goal is to acclimate Anthony to as many foods and substances as possible. I don't want to worry if he gets a wheat cracker or a glass of milk.

We've seen success stories in our own family. My cousin was lactose intolerant, but can now have dairy products without an allergic reaction. Another cousin had chronic sinus infections, congestion and drip. One day, as she drove home after an NAET treatment clearing Vitamin C allergies, her ears began to pop. With that the sinus drip started drying up. This has continued, improving her entire health outlook. Another cousin had a latex allergy that required her dentist to alter his methods of treatment. Dentists and dental hygienists routinely wear latex gloves. Once NAET treatments cleared latex, my cousin went to the dentist, told him to wear latex gloves, and she had no reaction at all.

For more information on NAET you can go to www.naet.com. Also Dr.Nambudripad has written a book explaining the treatment, and it is specifically aimed at the autism community: "Say Good-Bye to Allergy–Related Autism."

Appendix III
Hyperbaric Oxygen Therapy (HBOT)

This is a therapy where the entire body is treated with an atmosphere of pure, or nearly pure, oxygen with a pressure higher than that of normal atmospheric pressure (the air pressure measured by a barometer). Normal atmospheric pressure at sea level is 14.7 pounds per square inch. This is the weight of the air in the atmosphere upon everything below it. In other words, as walk through our lives there is always about 14.7 pounds of pressure on each square inch coming from above us. It sounds like a heavy load, but humans, and all living things, are used to it. All of life evolved under such pressure, and in many ways it shapes our world.

Hyperbaric Oxygen Therapy (HBOT) is conducted in a chamber where the body is intermittently treated with oxygen at increased pressure levels. The normal 14.7 pounds is called "one atmospheric pressure absolute" or 1 ATA. When a person is treated with HBOT this is increased to as much as 2 ATA, or double normal pressure, and the atmosphere exerting that pressure is nearly all oxygen. Oxygen levels in HBOT vary from 96% to 100%. The oxygen level of the air we breathe is less than 20%. This combination of concentration and pressure elevates the oxygen in bodily fluids and tissue to as much as 20 times its normal level. This increases the flow of oxygen even to those areas affected by blockages in blood flow.

You enter the HBOT chamber for up to an hour at a time. It's big enough to accommodate a mom and her child. It's an easy process. Really all you are doing is exposing yourself and your child to a different kind of atmosphere. You can bring in books, DVDs, puzzles—whatever will occupy you for an hour. After you've entered the operator pressurizes the chamber at whatever level necessary, also feeding in the oxygen to bring it to the proper purification. The level of oxygen is related to the pressure. Higher pressure chambers can be 100% oxygen. Lower pressure chambers are 96% oxygen. The higher pressure chamber does have limits in the amount of therapy that can be done due to oxygen toxicity. The body can only absorb so much oxygen, so this is closely monitored.

Dr. Julie Buckley has researched HBOT as it applies to autistic children. In her article in the November 2005 issue of *Medical Veritas: The Journal of Medical Truth* she cites scans where the effects of HBOT on the brain were monitored using Single Photo Emission Computed Tomography (SPECT). Dr. Buckley describes SPECT scans done before and after 40 sessions of Mild Hyperbaric treatments (MHBOT). These were treatments using 1.3 to 1.5 ATA, and 21% to 40% oxygen, much lower than the full treatments. These scans showed "dramatic improvements of cerebral brain flow" in the children involved, improvements that were maintained over time. Dr. Buckley felt that these studies needed to be researched further but the initial findings are very promising. Her article is at www.usautism.org/PDF_files_newsletters/j_buckley_md_hbot_article.pdf. Her website for more information is www.pppvonline.com.

I know of two types of HBOT chambers. One is a portable, vinyl chamber, which can be setup anywhere, even the home. The other is a steel chamber in which you wear a hood during the treatment to allow for higher concentrations of oxygen. Dr. Neubrander has an HBOT chamber in his office and he reports beneficial effects.

Some autistic children seem to benefit from the therapy. The theory is that areas deep in the brain are oxygenated. Some recent reports indicate that the pressurized oxygen can release stem cells from bone marrow in the body. The stem cells then regenerate brain tissue. A patient may undergo such treatments up to several times per week, with a physician monitoring the therapy and its effects.

Appendix IV
Chelation

One of the most prevalent theories about the dramatic increase in autism in the last 15 years involves children's reactions to heavy metals in the body and blood. One culprit is mercury, which has been used in vaccines, and also may come from other sources. DAN doctors remove these metals through the process of chelation. This involves introducing a drug known as a "chelator." As I have described in the book, the heavy metals bind to this drug, and it carries the metals out of the body. Once this is done the child receives glutathione, a supplement which acts like a mop, soaking up the metals.

Imagine the mercury as sand at the bottom of the bucket. It is all settled there, and the water above it is clear. The chelator goes in and stirs up the sand and starts to shake it all up. In a child's body mercury has settled deep in the bodies tissues. The chelator stirs it all up, just as the mop stirs up the sand. It grabs most of the floating metal, then the glutathione comes in and mops up more of the free flowing mercury. Glutathione is not a chelator by itself. It aids the chelation process, helping to detoxify the child. There are several ways to administer chelators. These include transdermal (through the skin), suppositories, oral, and with the use of an IV. There are also several types of chelators. These are identified by initials such as DMSA, TD-DMPS, and EDTA. For chelation you should go to a DAN doctor.

David Kirby wrote a fine book on metals and chelation called: "Evidence of Harm." Some say that chelation when done orally can cause more intestinal problems, allowing yeast to grow. One school of thought says to first strengthen the gut through diet (supplements, anti-fungals, probiotics and digestive enzymes), and only then perform chelation. The other opinion is that the mercury is causing all the problems in these children. Other symptoms, such as gut and methylation issues, are a response to the mercury, and it must be removed from the body before the child can improve. I chose a direct transdermal route with Anthony because I felt that there couldn't be any long-term improvement until the metals were out of my son. I believe the mercury impairs the neurological system, which affects everything. With Anthony all the lighter metals, such as nickel, arsenic, lead, antimony, came out first, but it took a year before he started to excrete Mercury. This is normal. As we did the chelation we took blood and urine tests every 8 weeks. They showed him dumping the light metals, then finally the mercury.

You might think of the mercury as being like a tick burrowed deep into the scalp, and the lighter metals as being the hair around it. You have to get out hair before you can remove the tick.

Appendix V
Jimmy's Story

In Chapter Fourteen I wrote about Jimmy, an 8-year-old boy I'd met outside the supermarket. I met him and his mother right after a short grocery run where I'd seen a milestone in Anthony's progress. He had been so good in the store, something I hadn't been sure about up to then. I'd felt a bittersweet pang when Jimmy's mother had said that she'd assumed Anthony was a typical boy. I'd been proud of my son, but I'd also seen that Jimmy was still caught in the grip of autism.

Over the next year-and-a-half I saw Jimmy occasionally, sometimes running into him and his mother in a store, other times catching a glimpse of them from my car. After each of these instances he haunted my thoughts. When I saw his eyes I realized that this boy was losing his battle with autism. Those eyes revealed an adorable, yet tortured soul. I could feel and see Jimmy's potential, yet what could I do?

About that time Anthony started into a program of Namburidad Allergy Elimination Treatment (NAET). My friend, Laura, had persuaded our NAET practitioner to participate in a study for children with Autism. Our job was to find children to get into the study.

"What about that boy you talk about, the one you met at the supermarket?" Laura asked me.

"Jimmy?"

"I'm sure he'd be a good subject."

"I see them all the time," I said. "I'll ask his mother."

Within a few days I got Laura in touch with Jimmy's mom, and after hours of persuasive phone calls, Laura got her to agree to get Jimmy the treatments. After that I saw Jimmy at the NAET practitioner's every week. Seeing him still depressed me. Even after all this time he couldn't use any words functionally. His communications skills were stuck at the level of pulling people toward whatever it was that he wanted. A big (well over 5', and 150 pounds) 8-year-old boy, Jimmy was also lovable. But his mother had run into roadblock after roadblock in traditional education, and felt the world had given up on her son. Jimmy made a fair amount of academic progress with a private therapist at home, but when his mom brought this to the attention of his school's authorities they dismissed her account. She taped the sessions with the therapist. The tapes showed Jimmy pointing at the right pictures when given the corresponding words. Teachers at his school said he was being prompted from off camera.

Jimmy's is one of many cases where school systems get locked into negative attitudes. Once they see a diagnosis of autism they make a whole set of assumptions about capabilities. Seldom are all, or even most, of these assumptions true. This guarantees that Jimmy's future will be terribly limited if left to the traditional educational institutions.

Once Jimmy and his mother started coming in for NAET I began explaining Verbal Behavior.

"With VB he can learn functional communication," I said.

"How do you define 'functional'?" his mom asked.

"Well, it's great that he can point at the word 'apple', but does he need an apple? Jimmy probably has some pretty good ideas about the things he really wants and needs, but he can't communicate them. Say he's thirsty and wants a glass of water. Right now that just sits there in his head unless he can actually see where the water is, or knows where it is beforehand. But if he understands that there has to be water somewhere nearby, and knows a way to communicate his need, that's functional."

"And you could teach him to do that?"

"I can try," I said.

She nodded. "I'd like that, and I'm sure Jimmy would like it too."

So Jimmy started visiting our home, and, as his mom watched, I began pairing with him. Pairing can take longer with an older child because that child may have had a lot more negative experiences with teachers.

Jimmy paired with me quickly. He is highly motivated by food, so I started with small pieces of his favorite treats. I paired the food with other activities: the trampoline, the TV, and a seesaw at the park. We worked on his behavioral issues. Jimmy constantly grabbed for food, but with help he did that less and less. Soon we began manding. When I found he could echo words, I skipped the sign language stage. He picked up on manding quickly, using words for chip, pop, bounce, juice, and water. He took to the concept of: "I talk, I get".

Even his therapist was impressed. Jimmy seemed happy as his inappropriate behaviors receded. I still work with Jimmy, and I see improvement all the time. His is a perfect example of how a child of any age can improve with VB.

Appendix VI
I Love You... Come Back to Me
By Laura Errera

After the birth of our son, Rocco, his first year was perfectly normal. He was reaching his milestones, and developing just as we had expected. His progress was so normal that it played a large role in our decision to have a second child. Everything seemed right.

Many children who suffer from autism start this way, not showing any atypical signs until they are past their first birthday. It was between 12 and 18 months that Rocco began showing symptoms.

I learned that I was pregnant about the same time I started seeing problems with Rocco. As these increased, and my pregnancy progressed, I couldn't eat, sleep or think. All I could do was vomit. I saw my son faltering, and there was my daughter growing within me. Then when Rocco was 18½ months we got the diagnosis. Now I knew I was seeing my son descending into autism's black hole. All his advances had faded along with our dreams.

That night I went online, and typed "recovering from autism" into the Search box. No one could tell me there wasn't a way to bring Rocco back; I was sure of that. I spent the next 36 hours researching how to save my son. That week I started reading books and articles—everything I could get my hands on. I felt like Rocky Balboa training for a fight.

Though I was truly inspired, I also felt terribly alone. Finally I sat down with my husband to talk it all out. I knew I had married a great guy who could stand up to a lot of uncertainties, but I also knew we were facing something that can tear a marriage apart. In my research I'd learned that the divorce rate among parents of autistic children is sky high. But I had done my homework about ways to attack the disease as well. I'd seen the possibilities of reversing Rocco's downward plunge. It wouldn't be simple or easy. I knew that the approach of biomedical interventions and Verbal Behavior methods would take everything we had, both emotionally and financially. The commitment was huge, but at least I was able to define it. I didn't want to lose my husband in the process of recovering our son. If I could show him the obstacles before we faced them I knew we could do it.

The interventions we've done with Rocco are similar to the ones Christie has outlined in this book. Rocco and I were already paralleling the Burnetts' experience when I met Christie. Nonetheless I was only starting down the road, and that beginning was the lowest point of my life. I hadn't seen any triumphs yet. All I'd seen was the disease itself. I was desperate for hope.

I met Christie through a therapist we shared. She saved my life. Suddenly here was a positive voice coming from someone who was doing so many of the same things I was. Here was a kindred soul who could both inspire me, and help me find the core of inspiration within myself. Here was another little boy facing the same darkness my son was facing. We weren't alone. Not only that, but the voice that was joining us was one that cheered us on.

That doesn't mean that the road has been easy or perfect. So far our outcomes have not been the same. Anthony came back to Christie, but Rocco hasn't fully returned. We've made progress, but complete recovery is still more dream than reality. Such different results shouldn't be unexpected, nor should they keep parents from trying. Autism is a huge, daunting puzzle, and doesn't get solved all at once. Also, not every solution is complete. Rocco and Anthony's cases show that the same interventions can produce different results. Some things that work for one child won't work for another.

My belief is that the damage to Rocco began with an undiagnosed autoimmune problem when he was an infant. I think that this problem manifested itself in invisible ways as he received various vaccines, culminating with the MMR and Chicken Pox vaccine that he got on his first birthday. This autoimmune problem joined with metal toxicity and viral issues from the vaccines, so that each shot compounded the problem until Rocco was ultimately beset by autism.

If only I'd known then what I know now! Sometimes I blame myself for not knowing that I didn't have to vaccinate my child on the exact schedule that my doctor gave us. I am haunted by the thought that I inadvertently caused my son's autism.

The interventions we've done have had good results. Though recovery is far from complete, Rocco is not as much a prisoner of autism's shadows as he was. When I first changed him over to a GFCF, soy-free diet my son began to point again, something he had done when he was younger, but had stopped doing. This told me I was on to something, so I kept going. After going to a DAN doctor we ordered tests. The results of these helped us define which interventions to do, and how to best target them. As Christie's story shows, there is no magic bullet. You have to try the things that seem to make sense, and continue with those that work.

In Rocco's case certain interventions have proved to be "big guns." These include Methyl B-12 shots, amino acids, essential fatty acids (cod liver oil), SCD (specific carbohydrate diet), lipoglutathione, digestive enzymes, probiotics, bethanthancol, chelation and Verbal Behavior therapy. Christie has covered most of these in this book.

As I've said, there are many differences between Anthony's case and Rocco's. My son is a "viral kid" meaning there are live viruses present in his body. I believe vaccines caused these. It's the only explanation for him having the measles virus in his gut. I am still trying to address this with bethanacol, large amounts of vitamin A and anti-virals like lauricidin.

The damage to Rocco's gut is severe, a common condition in autistic kids. Rocco's stomach is still healing, and the SCD diet is the greatest factor in this. I encourage anyone to try the dairy-free version of this diet. The diet turned Rocco's severe runs to formed stools for the first time in two years.

Since just before Rocco turn two I've been following the DAN protocol. It has taken him a long way, but not to full recovery. To reach that point I have researched compliments to the protocol. Recently we began the IV treatments of PK flush and glutathione three times per week. As Rocco's body detoxifies I am encouraged by some amazing results. We will continue with this until our doctor decides Rocco is ready for IV chelation. Once we've rid Rocco's body of metals we plan to do hard chamber H-BOT.

We have been chelating for almost three years with TD-DMPS. It took a year and a half for his metals to begin to move. If I could do this over I would start the IV protocol earlier. My advice is to research Patricia Kane's protocol. It has recovered many children. Be sure the doctor is well versed in her specific protocol.

There is no way around the fact that Rocco is a "tough to fix" kid, but it is also indisputable that we have made progress. A child's recovery depends on many factors but the most important one is the parents. I have counseled too many parents who have said, "I can't do that diet. It's too hard," or, "I can't get my child to take those vitamins." Parents must remember that if they give up, it is the child who will suffer. I know that I will fully recover Rocco.

As a parent you must do what you have to do. Don't give up if your child doesn't reach every predicted milestone. Keep going. Each intervention will bring you a piece of the puzzle, some bigger, some smaller. If I had quit my son would be condemned to a lifetime of silence. Instead he speaks. That alone would make it worth it, but I know that he can go on from there, so I continue doing all that I can. This is my message, and Christie's too: This is your child, so you must decide what makes sense. Ultimately you will live with the outcome as will your child. Don't listen to naysayers.

Remember: all too easily autism can be a lonely, isolating existence. Reach out to others who are facing the same trauma. Go online for support. We have a group of about 20-to-25 women who meet at a restaurant once a month to talk. We share what we are doing with our kids and help and support each other.

Christie saved my life. We have both met and reached out to lots of people through networking. We've each found some friends on our own, while discovering some through each other. Sharing is the key to success, and also to sanity. Before this I seldom asked for help from anyone, but now I leave my name and number everywhere. Autism taught me that. The autism community is more helpful than I could have ever imagined.

There is some residual sadness. Most of our friends "before autism" don't understand what it is like to live with this day-to-day. But that is balanced by the fact that we have many new friends, with Christie at the top of the list.

Through her, and so many others, I have learned, and Rocco has taken steps toward recovery. He has a long way to go but I will never give up on him. The process is expensive and draining, but not as difficult as taking care of your child for the rest of his life. I always want to lay my head down at night knowing I am doing all I can to help him. If you do the same for your child, you won't ever look back and wonder: "What if..."

Appendix VII
Alphabet Soup – A Recipe for Autism Recovery
By Regina Cioffi

After a very difficult pregnancy my son, Thomas, was born. Fifteen months later he was diagnosed with autism. When the neurodevelopmental pediatrician gave me this diagnosis he cautioned me not to waste time with biomedical approaches. He said I should concentrate on Applied Behavioral Analysis (ABA) therapy. I took the doctor at his word and for the next year I threw myself into studying ABA, physical therapy and occupational therapy.

A year after Thomas was diagnosed I attended a seminar about Applied Behavior Analysis/Verbal Behavior (ABA/VB) given by Alexis Higgins. It was at here that I met Christie Burnett and Laura Errera. Shortly thereafter Christie invited me to her house to meet with a group of other mothers of children with autism.

I have a saying: Autism is a disease of isolation. When my son was diagnosed with autism I gradually came to suffer from my own version of the disease, something I call "reverse autism". Reverse autism also works in reverse of hereditary diseases – you get it from your child. You stop going to neuro-typical (NT) events (the kinds of activities most of us do every day) and withdraw into your own world.

Once autism enters your life nothing you and your child do—therapies, doctor appointments, special diets etc.—is familiar to any of your friends. Because of this you don't share the things you once shared with others, and friendships fade, or sink into hibernation. You try to talk to others, but you realize you can't communicate. A wall has formed. You begin to feel misunderstood. Before you know it you are isolated.

Self-isolation, like any isolation, is lonely. By the time Christie asked me to her house loneliness had become a permanent part of my world. I realized I needed friends. As I went to this meeting of moms I felt hope for the first time in months.

When I got there I immediately felt welcomed. Christie is an unfailingly kind hostess. Her home is filled with the joy, love and loudness of a happy family. All the moms there were affected by it. As we began to talk about our experiences I felt a kinship with these other moms. I started talking to Laura. She mentioned that she and Christie liked it when moms "do biomedical" with their autistic children. I didn't have the faintest idea what she meant, but I knew I wanted her and Christie to be my friends, so I just shook my head up and down and pretended I understood.

Luckily Laura didn't stop there. She gave me the names of some books to read. The next day I went online to look for the books and found a website sale. I ordered "Children With Starving Brains" by Jacqueline McCandless and "Breaking The Vicious Cycle" by Elaine Gottschall, then got a great discount on their selection: "Natural Medicine Guide to Autism" by Stephanie Maharon.

These three books were the start of my recipe for alphabet soup. Every therapy I tried had an acronym: VB, SCD, CST, NAET, HR, EFT—you've run into most of them here in this book. I felt as if I'd heated a can of alphabet soup, and was looking down into the letters. The metaphor might seem trivial, but the unique combination of therapies I found for Thomas has brought him so close to full recovery that most people who meet him for the first time have no idea that autism might play a role in his life. Thomas continues to improve and I have high hopes for him.

I owe a great deal to Christie and Laura for helping Thomas and me find the path to healing. If I had never gone to that VB seminar where I met them I am not sure where my son would be at this point. Once they pointed me in the right direction I became an enthusiastic researcher into all things biomedical. That research has led me to new diets and supplements, and I have also discovered the "energy" medicines such as acupuncture, homeopathy and holographic re-patterning. All of these have helped Thomas.

I'd like to share the alphabet soup for autism recovery that worked with my son. Below are the therapies we found most helpful. The acronyms are followed by the words they represent, and a small *soupcon* of what each intervention contains. I also provide a book name or a website URL so you can do your own research to determine if the intervention will help your child. We have a saying in the autism world: "If you've seen one autistic child ... you've seen one autistic child." Every child is different and you know your child's needs best.

A1, DAN!, NAA – These stand for AutismOne, Defeat Autism Now! and the National Autism Association respectively. Join any or all of these national organizations to get the latest details on currently available autism treatments. Each of these organizations holds conventions where you can get cutting-edge treatment information and talk to parents who are on the same path as you.

SCD – Specific Carbohydrate Diet. This diet is well covered in "Breaking The Vicious Cycle" by Elaine Gottschall. You can also find information at www.pecanbread.com or www.breakingtheviciouscycle.com. SCD is absolutely necessary for every autistic child. Start slowly and wait for the gut to heal before introducing new foods. My son was on the diet for over two years before his gut healed enough that I could introduce new foods, but it was worth it. Now he eats well and has gained enough weight that he is over the 50th percentile for his age group in height and weight.

CST – CranioSacral Therapy. "CranioSacral Therapy" by John Upledger, D.O. www.upledger.com
This intervention works well with children who are very sensory seeking. If your child stands on his head, grinds his teeth, pushes his jaw into you, or seeks deep pressure in

other ways, this is the intervention to try. Find a practitioner who has been to the Upledger training (the website has a listing of trained practitioners). My practitioner was also a chiropractor as well as a Certified Clinical Nutritionist. That benefited my son tremendously.

VB – Verbal Behavior. "Verbal Behavior" by B. F. Skinner also "Teaching Language to Children with Autism" by Mark Sundberg and James Partington. www.behavioranalysts.com or www.difflearn.com
Christie did an excellent job in this book of describing the benefits of VB, and I have one more to add. If you have behavioral control of your autistic child, you will be able to successfully implement all other therapies. I can't stress enough how learning to do behavioral interventions with my son allowed all the various practitioners to work with him effectively. He sits to be examined, he cooperates during treatment, and this often results in excellent outcomes for the therapy modalities I use with him. Learn how to "pair" people and environments with your child. Learn how to use the "Accepting No" procedure for when you are at a practitioner's office and can't provide an item you child has manded for. Christie explains the educational benefits of VB, and I'll add that it helps your child develop the ability to enter real world venues such as restaurants, doctor's offices, playgrounds, and so many other places and situations.

NAET – Nambudripad's Allergy Elimination Technique "Say Goodbye To Allergy-Related Autism" by Dr. Devi S. Nambudripad. www.naet.com
Most autistic children suffer from various allergies, which in turn aggravate their symptoms of autism. The best book I have found to explain this is "Is This Your Child?" by Dr. Doris Rapp. NAET alleviates allergy symptoms so children can sleep better at night, increase the number of foods in

their diet, relieve respiratory allergies or skin rashes, help unclog their ears, and remove the "fog" they exist in due to chemical and food sensitivities.

One of the best things about NAET is the ability to "muscle test" food, clothes or any item, to see if your child is allergic to it. Once you learn this technique, which is based on kinesiology, you will be able to determine ahead of time if your child can eat or touch something. Instead of waiting until they are sick or have a reaction, you can prevent these things. If the muscle testing reveals an allergy, you can use NAET techniques to clear the allergy so that your child doesn't have to spend a lifetime in deprivation.

NAET also can be used to clear "emotional" blockages that can lead to allergies. I have used NAET to treat my son to allergies to people and places where he had a bad experience (example the phlebotomist's office) so he doesn't wind up with emotional disturbances that he will drag around the rest of his life.

Other parts of the alphabet:

I also use some energy approaches such as Acupressure, EFT – Emotional Freedom Technique, infant massage, Brain Gym, chiropractic, Holographic Repatterning, HADO, kinesiology, and Listening Therapy. A good website for these is www.mercola.com

I am currently trying something called "B-DORT" which stands for "Bi-Digital O-Ring Testing". It is a way to diagnose health issues and muscle test (using magnetic resonance) to see if a food or piece of clothing will cause a negative reaction in a person. It also has the ability to detoxify the body, and something everyone with autism needs.

You can also try Dance Therapy, Interactive Metronome, AIT or Tomatis, Homeopathy, Vibrational

Remedies, Essential Oils, Reikki, Feng Shui, yoga, meditation, or any spiritual endeavor. Do your research on the web and find something that is relaxing, relieves stress and is fun to do. Something as simple as piano lessons can have great benefit to your child.

The last ingredient in my recipe is to find people like Christie and Laura who "get" you and your child. A support system is crucial to getting through the day. Reach out to others in the autism community. Have a mom's night out periodically. Friends are the spice in the alphabet soup of autism recovery.

BIBLIOGRAPHY

Books:
Gottschall, Elaine, *Breaking the Vicious Cycle: Intestinal Health through Diet*, Kirkton Press, Ltd., Baltimore, Ontario, Canada 1994.

Hamilton, Lynn, Facing Autism: Giving Parents Reasons for Hope and Guidance for Help, Waterbrook Press, 2000.

Kirby, David, *Evidence of Harm: Mercury in Vaccines and the Autism Epidemic: A Medical Controversy*, St, Martin's Press, New York 2005.

Lewis, Lisa, *Special Diets for Special Kids*, Future Horizons, New York 1998.

Maurice, Catherine, *Let Me Hear Your Voice: A Family's Triumph over Autism*, Ballantine Books, New York, 1994.

McCandless, Jacquelyn, *Children with Starving Brains: A Medical Treatment Guide for Autism Spectrum Disorder*, Second Edition, Bramble Books, 2003.

Seroussi, Karyn, *Unraveling the Mystery of Autism and Pervasive Developmental Disorders: A Mother's Story of Research and Discovery*, Simon & Schuster, New York, 2000.

Shaw. Dr. William, *Biological Treatments for Autism and PDD*, Sunflower, 2001.

Skinner, B.F., *The Behavior of Organisms*, An Experimental Analysis, D. Appleton & Company, New York 1938.
Science and Human Behavior, Free Press, New York 1953.
Verbal Behavior, Appleton-Century-Crofts, Inc., New York 1957.

Sundberg, Mark L. and Partington, James W., *The Assessment of Basic Language and Learning Skills (The ABLLS): An assessment, curriculum guide, and skills tracking system for children with autism or other developmental disabilities.* Pleasant Hill, CA: Behavioral Analysts, Inc., 1998.

Websites:
www.autism.org -- Website serving as general resource for information about autism. Accessed 11/27/06.

www.autisme.net/candida1-uk.html -- The Candida Yeast Autism Connection, by Dr. Stephen M. Edelson. Accessed 11/27/06.

www.autismndi.com -- Website of Autism Network of Dietary Intervention, accessed 11/24/06.

www.autismwebsite.com/ARI/index_real.htm -- Website of the Autism Research Institute and their newsletter: Autism Research Review International. Accessed 11/27/06

www.chelationtherapyonline.com/articles/p106.htm -- Testimony of Dr. Stephanie Cave concerning mercury in vaccines, The House Committee on Government Reform in Washington, September 18, 2000. Accessed 11/27/06.

www.breakingtheviciouscycle.com -- Website started by the late Elaine Gottschall, dedicated to the SCD diet. Accessed 11/24/06.

www.childbrain.com -- Childbrain.com is the website of the Child Neurology and Developmental Center, the pediatric neurology practice of Rami Grossman, M.D.

www.danconference.com -- Website for current and future conferences of Defeat Autism Now! Accessed 11/24/06.

www.difflearn.com -- Website which is a source for ABA methods. Here you can find the ABLLS. Accessed 11/24/06.

www.drbuttar.com -- Website of Dr.Raschid A.Buttar, Vice Chairman, American Board of Clinical Metal Toxicology, North Carolina State University. Accessed 11/24/06.

www.drneubrander.com -- Website of Dr. James Neubrander with information about methyl-B12, and other biomedical methods. Accessed 11/24/06.

www.greatplainslaboratory.com -- Website of laboratory that does analysis for metals and other substances. Accessed 11/24/06.

www.justtomatoes.com -- Website for organic foods and recipes. Accessed 11/24/06.

www.kirkmanlabs.com -- Website for many nutritional supplements. Accessed 11/24/06.

www.poac.net -- Website for Parents of Autistic Children. Accessed 11/24/06.

www.pecanbread.com -- Website for many recipes that conform to the SCD diet. Accessed 11/24/06.

www.thoughtfulhouse.com -- Website dedicated to the recovery of children with developmental disorders, featuring Drs. Andrew Wakefield and Arthur Krigman, among others. Accessed on 11/27/06.

www.usautism,org/PDF_files_newsletters/j_buckley_md_hbot_article.pdf -- "How mild hyperbaric oxygen therapy works and why it is good for our children," by Dr. Julie Buckley, M.D. FAAP. Accessed 11/27/06.

www.vaccinesafety.edu/thi-table.htm -- A table showing how much thimerosol is in U.S.-licensed vaccines. Accessed 11/27/06

www.verbalbehaviornetwork.com -- Workshops, resources, and other assistance in learning and teaching Verbal Behavior methods. Accessed on 11/27/06.

Other:

"Abnormal Intestinal Permeability in Children with Autism," P.D.Eufemia et al, *Acta Paediatrica* 85(1996):1076

"A Case-Control Study of Mercury Burden in Children with Autistic Spectrum Disorders by Bradstreet J, Geier DA, Kartzinel JJ, Adams JB**, Geier MR. *Journal of American Physicians & Surgeons* 2003;8:76-79(in NAA Conference Manual by Bradstreet,and Geier)

DAN Conference Manuals

Autism: A Novel Type of Mercury Poisoning" *Medical Hypothesis* 56(4) 462-471(2001) Dr. Bernard Rimland et al.

Journal of Applied Behavior Analysis, journal resource for advances in Verbal Behavior, Washington State University, 1968-present.

"Enteroscopy: Another Piece in the Jigsaw of this Gut-brain Syndrome." Balzola F,et al. *American Journal of Gastroenterology*, April,2005

Wakefield A. Article abstract taken from 1998 Conference Proceedings "Psychobiology of Autism: Current Research and Practice. This taken from Biological Treatments for Autism and PDD by Dr.William Shaw pg 112

www.ingramcontent.com/pod-product-compliance
Lightning Source LLC
Chambersburg PA
CBHW031939110426

42744CB00028B/80